WITHDRAWN
University of
Illinois Library
at Urbana-Champaign

Communicating Public Access to Government Information

PROCEEDINGS OF
THE SECOND ANNUAL
LIBRARY GOVERNMENT DOCUMENTS
AND INFORMATION CONFERENCE

Communicating Public Access to Government Information

PROCEEDINGS OF
THE SECOND ANNUAL
LIBRARY GOVERNMENT DOCUMENTS
AND INFORMATION CONFERENCE

Edited by Peter Hernon
Graduate School of Library and
Information Science
Simmons College, Boston

MECKLER PUBLISHING
520 Riverside Ave., Westport, CT 06880

3 Henrietta Street, London WC2E 8LU, England

Library of Congress Cataloging in Publication Data

Library Government Documents and Information
    Conference (2nd : 1982 : Arlington, Va.)
    Communicating public access to government
information.

    "Held in Arlington, Virginia, on March 26 and
27, 1982"—Pref.
    Bibliography: p.
    1. Government publications—Library resources—
United States—Congresses.   2. Libraries—United
States—Special collections—Government publications
—Congresses.   I. Hernon, Peter.   II. Title.

Z7164.G7L5   1982   [Z1223.Z7]   025.17'34   82-14334
ISBN 0-930466-59-4

Copyright © 1983 Meckler Publishing (except where noted)

All rights reserved. No part of this publication may be
reproduced in any form without permission from the
publisher, except by a reviewer who may quote brief
passages in review.

Printed and bound in the United States of America

025.1734
L616c
1982

CONTENTS

vi   Contents

TABLES

FIGURES

PREFACE

The articles in this book are based on presentations delivered at the second Annual Library Government Documents and Information Conference sponsored by Meckler Publishing and held in Arlington, Virginia, on March 26 and 27, 1982. The purpose of this conference was to provide an opportunity for writers in the documents field to interact with practicing librarians, library educators, government officials, publishers, library science students, and others interested in the topic of government publications; and to offer a forum for detailed discussion of major issues—in this case, facets of public access to government publications/information produced in various formats (hardcopy/paper, machine-readable, and map).

The articles, written by government officials, librarians, and library educators, provide an opportunity to consider both practical and theoretical matters and to better merge theory with practice. Too often, documents librarianship has emphasized practice at the expense of theory. However, both are important and together can improve public access to government information. For example, the Government Printing Office and many documents librarians encourage the formulation of state plans to better meet the goals of the depository library program. Yet, they are encouraging statewide planning at a time when most of the depository libraries have not even engaged in planning at the institutional level.

First, depository libraries need to develop written collection development policies and to view collection development as a planning process operating within a subject context.[1] Only after such planning has been accomplished can meaningful planning take place at the state level. Collection development is a good example of the unification of theory and practice. It enables librarians to develop functional collections, emphasizing the selection and retention of the more highly needed source material, and to work toward the improvement of inter-institutional cooperation for the identification and rapid availability of those source materials in lesser demand.

As several of the articles point out, further research is needed if documents librarianship is to expand its theoretical base and if documents librarians are to base their decisions on more than opinion, supposition, and informal discussions with clientele, publishers, and other groups. However, it should be recognized that there are too few researchers in the documents field, that the present level of funding is insufficient to conduct many of the needed studies, and that many documents librarians do not fully appreciate the value of research.[2] All of these problems merit attention. It is my hope that this conference and these proceedings will result in a discussion of such problems and their implications for the further development of documents librarianship.

The concept of "documents to the people" reflects an interest in understanding public access and in communicating to the public the suggestion that government publications housed in libraries may meet many of their information needs. With this in mind, the following nine chapters examine various facets of access and make pertinent observations and recommendations.

Bernadine E. Abbott Hoduski encourages documents librarians to influence decision-making by government publishers, printers, distributors, and indexers, as well as by those who create and interpret policies governing public documents. Librarians can be influential because they seek services and information for users of government information and not for themselves. Both the general public and government officials, she finds, perceive librarians as being impartial in providing information services.

Joseph F. Caponio describes how the National Technical Information Service (NTIS), part of the U.S. Department of Commerce, specializes in providing public access to the results of federally funded research, development, planning, and engineering analyses. NTIS helps American businesses and industries to become more competitive in worldwide markets by channeling this specialized information (as well as technological innovations) to business, industry, government, and the public through a variety of products and services.

Brian Land examines public access from another perspective—the development of Freedom of Information legislation in Canada. He discusses Bill C-43, which has been in committee for more than a year, and makes comparisons, when appropriate, between the Canadian legislation and the U.S. Freedom of Information Act. Bill C-43 provides a statutory right to access to information in government records in accordance with the principle

that government information should be made available to the public, that necessary exceptions to the right of access should be limited and specific, and that decisions on the disclosure of information should be reviewed independently of government.

Kathleen M. Heim, who explores the existing social science information system, notes that information in machine-readable form is inaccessible to all but the most sophisticated and heavily funded researchers. Libraries and information centers, she finds, have largely failed to provide access—bibliographical or actual—to this vital part of the social science information system. It is her belief that documents librarians should function as bibliographical brokers of government machine-readable statistical data through government units cooperating with the Interagency Committee on Data Access and Use.

An estimated eighty percent of all currently produced maps are published by governmental bodies, ranging from those at the international level to those at the municipal level. Charles A. Seavey, who examines some of these products of governmental bodies, points out the information value of the cartographic format. He suggests that the development of government map collections is less advanced than it is for other governmentally produced information formats.

Michael L. Tate, who examines government publications relating to American Indians, demonstrates the disunity of federal policy toward Native Americans and how the publications of federally created task forces have led to pernicious legislation. He also draws attention to the inconsistency of federal agencies (and thus, their publications) in defining just who is an Indian, and the Bureau of Indian Affairs' discouragement of research into post-World War II records. Both of these problems are of great concern to today's Indian population because they have brought confusion to treaty-entitlement programs and the preparation of litigation on behalf of tribal governments. Finally, Tate highlights the possibility of a more hopeful future brought about through the recommendations of American Indian Policy Review Commission.

A discussion of public access and the quality of information content would not be complete without an examination of reference service provided by depository libraries. General reference service in academic, public, and special libraries has been the subject of "unobtrusive" testing, whereby proxies, posing as clientele, ask questions requiring factual or bibliographic information and score library staff members on the number of correct responses. Such studies have shown that reference librarians answer approximately half of the questions correctly, and that they frequently do not make referrals outside the library. Peter Hernon and Charles R. McClure apply unobtrusive testing to staff members of academic depository libraries. Their test results show some similarities between the results of assessing general library reference service and documents service. However, the data suggest that in most instances the probability of obtaining a correct answer for U.S. government documents-related questions is less than that reported for general reference service.

With one theme of these proceedings being the need for additional research, it is appropriate that John V. Richardson looks at the nature of research in the documents field, specifically research derived from specialization papers, theses, and doctoral dissertations accepted by North American library schools. He examines basic characteristics of graduate research (e.g., the names of influential advisers and the level of government explored) and postulates that the coming years may see a decline in such research.

The final chapter, by Gary R. Purcell, reinforces the themes emphasized in this preface and attempts to show the relationships among the previous eight chapters. Purcell points out that documents librarians need to be aware of public access and the availability of source material in nonprint formats. In this regard, he sees a major role for library school education.

The conference and these proceedings constitute an effort to allow practicing librarians an opportunity to step back from their daily tasks and to examine various facets of public access to government publications not fully developed in the published literature and, perhaps, not well covered at other conferences. We must all work together to ensure public access (bibliographic control, physical accessibility, ease of access to source material held in depository collections, quality reference service, etc.) to the range of government publications/information that would meet diverse information needs.

Peter Hernon
Simmons College, Boston
June 1982

References

1. *See* Peter Hernon and Gary R. Purcell, *Developing Collections of U.S. Government Publications* (Greenwich, CT: JAI Press, forthcoming).

2. *See* Peter Hernon, "Documents Librarianship in the 1980s: Current Issues and Trends in Research," *Government Publications Review*, 9 (1982): 99-120.

POLITICAL ACTIVISM FOR DOCUMENTS LIBRARIANS

By Bernadine E. Abbott Hoduski

Introduction

Librarians can and do influence government publishers, printers, distributors, and indexers of government information. Librarians also influence those who create and interpret the policies governing these programs. They have influence because they speak not for themselves but for the citizens who use government information.

Librarians are constantly under pressure from citizens to obtain needed information. Since librarians do not obtain the information for their own use, they have greater influence in dealing with government agencies. They are perceived by the public, government, and business as helpful to all and as being objective in extending their services; in one day they might help both the corporation and the agency or group suing that corporation. Jack Cherns, formerly of Her Majesty's Stationery Office, said, in an address at the 1978 IFLA conference, that

Librarians are virtually specialists in organized management of information, and uniquely able to take a broad view across a field of fragmented interests. Perhaps they could be considered as a professional body of opinion acting almost as guardians of the public interest in the provision of government information. There is no other kind of pressure group in the same field.[1]

© 1983 Bernadine E. Abbott Hoduski

Government agency staffs sometimes practically beg for input and support from the library community. For example, the National Technical Information Service (NTIS) realized that the COSATI rules for cataloging the technical reports in the *Government Reports Announcements* were outdated. They turned for help to a group called Information Hangups. Information Hangups not only worked with NTIS on revising the rules, but convinced NTIS and its cooperative cataloging partners in the "sci/tech" agencies to hire a contractor to resolve the differences in cataloging between NTIS and its partner agencies. The contract has since been expanded to include the compilation of a data-element dictionary, which will also include a comparison between MARC and COSATI. This may be the basis for a truly cooperative cataloging effort between NTIS and the Government Printing Office.

It might be useful at this point to present a good example of the influence that librarians have exerted on government publishing programs. In late 1976, a number of library groups asked the Joint Committee on Printing (JCP) to work on increasing the number of maps distributed through the Depository Library Program. The library groups identified a number of problems that complicated their efforts to develop map collections. Foremost among these problems were the following: they must deal with over a dozen separate agencies; they must wait for years to get into an agency depository system because each system can accommodate only a limited number of libraries; and finally, they do not get some maps at all and must pay for others.

In order to determine the interest of the approximately 1,300 libraries in the Depository Library Program in receiving maps, the Joint Committee on Printing asked the GPO to conduct a survey. The response indicated that the majority of depository libraries was indeed interested in receiving maps and wished to have the opportunity to select from among all Federal agencies those maps of interest in their area.

During 1977, 1978, and 1979, the Joint Committee on Printing took steps to persuade a number of agencies to make their maps available. The CIA agreed to provide its urban atlases and certain other maps; the Department of Agriculture agreed to provide farmland maps; and the Census Bureau agreed to provide all of its maps. The Joint Committee on Printing also began discussions with the Defense Mapping Agency.

Although progress has been made, the Joint Committee on Printing decided in 1980 to identify and secure those maps, not then being distributed, which the libraries regarded as most vital. The Joint Committee on Printing sought the advice of the Cartographic Users Advisory Council, which draws its members from the Map Round Table of the American Library Association, the Geography & Map Division of the Special Library Association, the Geoscience Information Society, and the Western Association of Map Libraries.

Next, the Joint Committee on Printing called together a number of the major map-producing agencies for a series of meetings in which the possibility of a joint distribution and indexing system was discussed. These agencies included the Department of Agriculture, the Department of the Interior, the Department of Commerce, the Defense Mapping Agency, the Federal Emergency Management Agency, the National Ocean Survey, the Library of Congress and the Government Printing Office. So far, the group has completed two studies, the first of which describes the depository systems run by the GPO, the Geological Survey, the National Ocean Survey, and the Defense Mapping Agency. The study shows that there is extensive overlap among the libraries served by these four map-distributing bodies. There are some seventy libraries in the United States that are receiving maps on deposit from all four bodies, and of these, fourteen are GPO Regional Depositories, which by law are required to receive and permanently retain all the documents they receive. The second study provides information on map production and distribution by the federal government.

The Joint Committee on Printing asked the GPO for a status report on its map distribution and cataloging efforts for 1980 and 1981. In that report, the GPO indicated that as a result of the JCP's visits to the GPO field printing and procurement offices, it is now ordering all agency maps procured through the GPO Regional Printing Procurement Offices to be distributed to depository libraries. So far, the GPO is not overseeing the print orders for maps produced in JCP-approved agency printing plants. Also at the JCP's suggestion, the GPO and the Library of Congress have begun a cooperative map cataloging program. It is hoped that this program will be extended to the Geological Survey and other map-producing agencies.

Another meeting of map-producing agencies is expected to be called. It is hoped that the group can be expanded to include the Army Corps of Engineers and others. There is still a great deal more to accomplish, but it is worthwhile pursuing. It will be more cost-effective if the duplicative efforts of the various federal agencies which distribute maps can be reduced. However, care must be taken to insure the public of access to all federal maps.

Political Activism

The following section discusses a number of ways in which librarians can exert influence.

Become a Policy Maker, Run for Political Office, or Aspire for High Appointive or Civil Service Office

Librarians can do it as well as anyone else. I spoke several years ago to a group of librarians, urging them to become politically active. I later heard from one of the librarians in the group. She said she was so inspired by my speech that she got a job with a congressman from her home district. When he retired, she decided to run for his seat. She was not elected. Nevertheless, she did not run in vain; she made a marked impression on the electorate. And even a defeated congressional candidate is treated with respect on the "Hill." Besides, having run looks great on a resumé. The important thing is to have the courage to try.

Take a Job with the Policy Makers

Librarians can work for a congressional committee, for a minister or secretary of a major department on the federal or local level, or become an assistant to a city mayor, state governor or city council member. My position on the Joint Committee on Printing is a good example. As Professional Staff Member for Library and Distribution Services, I am present when policies which will affect hundreds of libraries and citizen/users are decided. I am present when a bit of information or a well-placed suggestion will do the most good, *before* the regulation or the law is passed. I am present to initiate programs and studies which may benefit libraries and library users and which would not be thought of by nonlibrary staff.

For example, it is doubtful that anyone would have considered studying the *U.S. Congressional Serial Set* to determine if it is still the most effective and economical way to fulfill Congress's need to preserve its own documentation. At my suggestion, the Joint Committee on Printing established an advisory committee to study how the *Serial Set* could be improved. This study encompassed the physical format of the set, its contents, indexing access to the documents in it, and methods of lowering production costs. The advisory committee was composed of representatives from the JCP, the Government Printing Office, the Senate and House libraries, the Library of Congress, the National Archives Library and the depository library community. This committee of policy-makers, producers, and users worked together to improve the set.

The committee made a number of recommendations which were accepted by the Joint Committee on Printing. They included standardizing the set (i.e., preparing one version instead of two). Standardization which will reduce the cost from $57 per volume to $21 per volume, has saved at least $100,000 in fiscal years 1981 and 1982. In addition, 633 depositories have opted for microfiche and 350 for paper copy. During fiscal years 1981 and 1982, these measures have saved the taxpayers some 2.8 million dollars.

A more recent example of librarians' influence is in the area of the publishing of the Department of Education (DOE) indexes by the private sector. Many librarians wrote to the Joint Committee on Printing, complaining that the July to December cumulative index to *Resources in Education* was going to be published privately. The JCP began an investigation of the DOE's publishing activities and discovered that a number of publications were being published by private presses without a waiver from the Joint Committee on Printing. Late in 1981, Senator Charles Mac Mathias, Chairman of the JCP, wrote to Secretary Terrell H. Bell, directing him to publish *Resources in Education (RIE)* and *RIE Indexes*, the *ERIC Thesaurus*, and the *Current Index to Journals in Education* through the GPO. He also directed the Department of Education to provide microfiche copies of all the documents in the ERIC system that were produced by the DOE staff or were financed by DOE grants or contracts. These documents include about 500 titles per year. Distribution of them began early in 1982.

Write Your Own Legislation

Librarians can get sympathetic legislators to introduce legislation for them; this is done more and more frequently. Some recent examples include efforts by librarians in Maryland, Virginia, and North Carolina. Librarians in Virginia persuaded the legislature to revise an existing statute they did not like because it did not strongly direct the State Librarian to establish and support a depository system. The old statutory language said that the State Librarian *may* require an agency to deliver copies of state publications to the State Library and that the State Library *may* send copies of state publications to any university, college, public library, or society. The new legislation uses the word *shall* and directs the State Library to establish a depository system. Apparently, the State Library is taking its added responsibility seriously; it is issuing a shipping list along with the actual documents. Even more importantly, the State Library is requiring that depositories meet minimum requirements in the areas of organization, maintenance, and service to the public. It is also inspecting depositories to assure their compliance with the standards.

Librarians in North Carolina faced a situation in which there was no state documents depository system. After several years of extensive work, they persuaded the North Carolina Legislature to pass a bill setting up a depository system. This depository system benefits from a checklist that meets GODORT guidelines.

The endeavors in Virginia and North Carolina concentrated on getting tangible results. In Maryland the librarians adopted a different tactic. Under the able leadership of Ann Shaw Burgan of the Enoch Pratt Library, they persuaded the Maryland Legislature to pass a resolution (in May of 1979) directing the Governor to set up a task force on documents.

A broadly representative body was appointed by Governor Harry R. Hughes in January of 1980. The Governor's charge to the task force was "to study and evaluate the system of collecting, distribution & making accessible various state and local government publications & reports."

The task force met fourteen times between January 1980 and September 1981. It did a tremendous amount of work in a short time. First, it held two open meetings at which producers and users of documents discussed the issues. The task force then conducted two surveys. One went to state agencies to determine the type and quantity of publications they were producing. The other went to five hundred fifty libraries, colleges, universities, organizations, and user groups to determine the availability and accessibility of information about state publications and of the publications themselves.

The result of this work was a bill written by the task force, which was introduced into the Maryland House of Delegates on January 25, 1982 and into the Maryland Senate on January 27, 1982. It passed the House with one amendment. A hearing was held in the Senate. The Senate asked the task force if it would agree to an amendment. The task force announced that it would and the Senate voted on the bill in March.

One of the introducers of the well-written bill was a member of the task force. The bill sets up a state publication depository and distribution program as part of the State Library Resources Center, establishes a commission to oversee the administration of the program, outlines which libraries will be the initial members of the system, makes provision for the addition of other depositories, and requires a monthly listing of all state publications received for the program. The commission's constituency is interesting. It shall have nine members appointed by the Governor as follows: three members representing depository libraries, three members representing state agencies, and three members from the general public. The other interesting element of this bill is the definition of a state publication:

State publication means information materials produced, regardless of format, by the authority of, or at the total or partial expense of any state agency. It includes a publication sponsored by a state agency, issued in conjunction with, or under contract with the Federal government, local units of government, private individuals, institutions, corporations, research firms or other entities.

Work as a Librarian in a Government Agency

Librarians in government agencies are in a key position to influence the publishing, printing, and distribution policies of their agency. These librarians should study the methods of producing and distributing their agency's publications. They should get to know the printers, publishers, and authors of their agency's publications. Those who write, design, or decide that a publication should be produced, are eager to see it read. Librarians should advise them on the ways their publication can be made known to the public.

Librarians should offer expert advice when agency policies covering the indexing and distribution of publications are written. They should offer information about pertinent laws requiring indexing and they should offer to help write regulations and procedures which will assure that publications will get to the indexing operations. They should also incorporate these procedures in agency handbooks.

When a publication is cataloged or indexed it should be brought to the attention of the writer or editor. Librarians should point out to this person the value of having his/her work listed in a national bibliography or on-line network catalog. The agency librarian is in the best position to make sure that all of the agency's publications are cataloged and indexed in the proper places. If the agency's publications are not being included, the librarian should find out why and take steps to make sure they are.

Librarians should persuade their agencies to participate in cooperative cataloging programs with the major government indexing and cataloging agencies. Often agencies are not providing complete coverage because they have a shortage of staff. Herein is an advantage of cooperative cataloging.

Librarians should get involved in the creation of publications. They should provide their agency's publishers with information on standards for title pages, bibliographic citations, ID numbers, cataloging in publication programs, and bibliographies. They should offer to check footnotes in order to assure sufficient information for retrieval of the cited material. Librarians should also urge their agency to adopt bibliographic standards.

Identify and Share Marketing Information with Government Publishers

Librarians have marketing information which government publishers need, particularly in these days of cutbacks in publishing. Librarians know which publications are used; they hear from their users concerning the usefulness of publications. Agency publishers are interested in how many copies of their titles go to depository libraries, who reads them, and where the libraries are located. Agencies also expect to be able to send citizens to the libraries now that they must cut back on free distribution. Agencies are more willing to budget for copies of publications to go to libraries if they feel sure that citizens can actually use them. Some agencies have complained about the efforts of several depository libraries to charge user fees, and have asked the GPO and the Joint Committee on Printing to make sure that this does not happen.

Infiltrate the Publishers and Printers

Become a government publisher. If you cannot do that, attend meetings of publishers and printers. You might also volunteer to plan a program for a publishing or printing association, or participate in workshops directed at printers and publishers. A good example of a librarian joining a government printing establishment is Lewis Foreman, an English librarian, who joined Her Majesty's Stationery Office as head of the bibliographic service.

Learn to Speak Their Language

Librarians can take printing and publishing courses. Often the instructor will be a government employee. Librarians can visit printing and publishing establishments. When doing so, they should make an effort to see the new printing technologies such as electronic printers, laser printers, and word processors.

Educate Any Government Person Willing to be Educated about Bibliographic Control, Access, Depository Systems, Etc.

You never know when that person will be in a position to do some good for libraries.

React Quickly to Government Requests for Feedback on Government Policies and Regulations

Early in 1981, the Office of Management and Budget issued Bulletin 81-16: "Elimination of Wasteful Spending on Government Periodicals, Pamphlets and Audio Visual Products." Many librarians and associations have reacted to the bulletin and have worked to assure that useful and needed publications are not eliminated.

Volunteer Advice

When government advisory committees are set up, you should insist that a librarian serve on them. When the Joint Committee on Printing set up an advisory committee on the revision of Title 44, representatives of two library groups were included. This would not have happened if the librarians had not persisted in giving advice.

The advisory committees to the Government Printing Office did not just happen. Librarians insisted that the groundwork for an advisory committee on depository libraries be included in the 1962 depository law.

Get Government Committees to Investigate Printing and Publishing Activities

The Senate Governmental Affairs Committee, U.S. Congress, studied the publishing activities of agencies of the executive branch. The Committee asked for a complete list of all publications distributed to the public from January 1977 to June 1978. The list was to include information concerning the title, number of copies distributed, and channels used for distribution. It was found that 102,000 publications were distributed and that an estimated 36,000 publications were not listed in the *Monthly Catalog* for that time period. The raw data were turned over to the Joint Committee on Printing for further study. The Joint Committee on Printing used these data in its discussions with a number of the agencies that had assured the JCP that they were in compliance with Title 44. The Governmental Affairs Committee study showed otherwise.

Write Articles for Journals and Newsletters Read by Government Publishers, Printers, Policy-Makers and the Public

Since few of these people read library literature, librarians should try to get articles into the popular press. A number of librarians have managed to get their depository library services written up in their local newpapers. They have also written articles for college newsletters and other such publications.

Work with Other Groups to Influence Public and Government Opinion

The Government Documents Round Table (GODORT) of the American Library Association is working with the Society for History in the Federal Government on a study of the treatment of the GPO collection at the National Archives. The American Library Association is working with the Coalition to Save Our Documentary Heritage, which is trying to restore funding to the National Archives and is working for the separation of the National Archives from the General Services Administration.

Convince Agencies to Put on Training and Information Workshops for Librarians and Others

While you have the instructors captive, make suggestions for improvements in policies and procedures. The librarians at a documents workshop in Texas convinced the then head of the Office of the Federal Register, Fred Emery, to launch an educational program on how to use the *Federal Register*. Hundreds of workshops for anyone who wanted to use the *Federal Register* were subsequently held around the country. The Patent Office was asked to give a two-day workshop at the June 1979 ALA meeting. The librarians took that opportunity to ask the Patent Office to return its publications to the depository system.

Convince Government Publishers and Printers to Hire Librarians for Indexing and Accessing Projects

The Office of the Federal Register hired Carol Mahoney, a librarian, to improve the indexing to the *Code of Federal Regulations* (CFR). She has done a good job of improving the index and has developed a plan to get agency regulators to help index their regulations in the *Federal Register*. Information Handling Services hired Judy Russell to produce an index to all of the issues of the *CFR*. U.S. Historical Documents Press hired Edna Kanely, former editor of the *Monthly Catalog*, to add information, such as missing SuDoc numbers and additional subject access, to older issues of the *Monthly Catalog*.

Advertise Your Existence and Your Services

You might get government agencies to advertise for you. You might also ask agency field offices in your area to list the name of your library in their directories and newsletters.

When to Influence

Influence at the Creative Stage of Publishing

It is important to educate authors and editors as to what information should be included on a title page. Adequate information on the author and the publisher should be included. For example, often left out is the agency or subagency that actually did the work; sometimes forgotten are the information on the source of the publication and even the title page! Librarians should provide agencies with information on ANSI or other standard title pages, cataloging in publication programs, identification numbers (such as ISSN's, classification numbers, report numbers, and special ordering numbers), availability information, and addresses.

Librarians should point out the need for wide margins for rebinding; correct microfilming of large and double pages, maps and so on; and sturdy binding so that books will not fall apart with normal use. The Congressional Appropriation Committees made sure that depository libraries would continue to get hardbound copies of the *Congressional Directory* and *United States Code* even though other recipients were forced to get softbound copies.

Influence at the Bibliographic Control Stage

Librarians should try to convince agency staff to provide indexing for individual volumes. They should convince staff members to provide their publications to service agencies and libraries for cataloging purposes. In the United States, librarians have been successful in getting GPO cataloging into the AACR and MARC systems so that the cataloging can be incorporated into such computerized networking systems as OCLN and WLN, as well as such commercial systems as Lockheed Dialog and BRS.

Libraries are also cataloging state publications according to AACR and MARC, and a number of them are establishing the official names of government agencies for the Library of Congress in its NACO project.

Conclusion

This chapter has neither covered every way of influencing nor every area that needs influencing. Undoubtedly we can all think of others. Many librarians do not think of themselves as having the influence to shape the structure of the government information world. Librarians have tended to undervalue the expertise, knowledge, services and collections they have developed. But they must not underestimate their power to influence and shape the future of the information world. It is more important than ever for librarians to look out for the public's interests.

References

1. Jack Cherns, "Government Publishing—An Overview," Paper given to *International Federation of Library Associations and Institutions*, 44th Cong., Paper No. 16/Op/1E, 1978, p. 10.

THE NATIONAL TECHNICAL INFORMATION SERVICE IN THE 1980s

By Joseph F. Caponio

The theme of this conference, "Communicating Public Access to Government Information," is of vital interest to the National Technical Information Service. As most of you know, NTIS is part of a vast information transfer chain whose major links are the organizations represented at this conference.

This chapter will discuss "NTIS in the 1980s." Before it begins, however, I think it is appropriate to review the functions and responsibilities that were assigned to the Department of Commerce by the Congress when NTIS's predecessor organization, the Clearinghouse for Federal Scientific and Technical Information, was established.

Public Law 776 (81st Congress) stated that the purpose of the organization was

to provide for the dissemination of technological, scientific, and engineering information to American business and industry, and for other purposes.

To accomplish this task, the law further stated:

The Secretary of Commerce is hereby directed to establish and maintain within the Department of Commerce a clearinghouse for the *collection* and *dissemination* of scientific, technical, and engineering information.... To this end [he shall] take such steps as he may deem necessary and desirable—

(a) to search for, collect, classify, coordinate, integrate, record, and catalog such information from whatever sources, foreign and domestic, that may be available; and

(b) to make such information available to industry and business, to State and local governments, to other agencies of the Federal Government, and to the general public through the preparation of abstracts, digests, translations, bibliographies, indexes, and microfilm and other reproductions, for distribution either directly or by utilization of business, trade, technical, and scientific publications and services.

The Congress also included a provision in the law that was very unusual for a federal government organization (at least it *was* prior to the present administration). The provision stated:

It is the policy of the Act, to the fullest extent feasible, and consistent with the objectives of this Act, that each of the services and functions provided herein shall be self-sustaining or self-liquidating and that the general public *shall not* bear the cost of publications and other services which are for the special use and benefit of private groups and individuals.

As is the case with most legislation, many interpretations can be made of this provision. The real interpretive decisions come, however, from the Office of Management and Budget (OMB), which must approve or disapprove requests for appropriated funds. Since 1972, the OMB has consistently interpreted the provision to mean that NTIS cannot receive any appropriated funds to offset overall operating costs.

This interpretation results in a unique responsiblity for the NTIS to recover all the costs of its operations from the users of its information products and services, thereby precluding the need for appropriated funds (i.e., *tax dollars*).

Until now we have discussed the general mandated requirements, constraints, and policies that form the basis for the overall operation of NTIS. Let us now turn our attention to the product lines NTIS offers.

The basic NTIS products are scientific and technical research reports produced by or for the federal government. They amount to a large volume of documents—about twice as many titles as the entire U.S. book industry publishes each year.

The NTIS report collection includes acquisitions from the National Aeronautics and Space Administration, the Departments of Defense, Energy, Commerce, Health and Human Services, and more than two hundred other federal agencies. NTIS makes over 1.3 million different publications available, none of which is ever out of print. In 1981 nearly six million copies were sold to some 100,000 customers.

When government agencies send their technical reports to NTIS, it in turn catalogs, indexes, and abstracts them, as well as keys them into its computer, and microfilms them. The indexes are maintained under computer control. The data base can be accessed by the public, either directly or through any one of several commercial computerized bibliographic information vendors. After reviewing the computer results or any of the other NTIS bibliographic and announcement media, a customer may request a copy of the particular report(s) needed, in either microform or hardcopy. NTIS bills the customer accordingly.

In the past, information was interpreted to mean ordinary technical publications, i.e., the journal, the article, or the technical report. It is interpreted *much* more broadly now, and as a result NTIS collects and disseminates other types of federal information products.

Two of these information products are *computer software* and *data files*, both of which have utility *beyond* their original functions. Computer programs for general use are now *required* to be sent to NTIS (technical reports are not; we must persuade agencies to send them to us). In addition, there has been a phenomenal increase in both the number and types of machine-readable data bases established by and for the government's own use. At the same time, many users are finding that the machine-readable data gathered, organized, and presented for one purpose can be *reorganized*, *re*-formatted and used *just as effectively* for *other* purposes. They are also finding that a number of data bases (or parts of some of them) can be merged into more comprehensive data bases. These augmented data bases are of greater value because they permit new and more extensive correlations and analyses.

Primarily, NTIS provides wholesaler-like support to information vendors, or others; it will refine data and programs according to customers' needs.

Currently NTIS is working on the four initial stages of this expanded program:

- Access by lease will be provided for bibliographic data files produced by federal agencies. Several agreements have been concluded for release of the following data bases:
  —*Selected Water Resources Abstracts* of the Department of Interior,
  —*U.S. Patent Full Text File, U.S. Patent Classification File, U.S. Patent Bibliographic File* of the Patent and Trademark Office,
  —*Summary of Projects Completed* of the National Science Foundation (NSF),
  —*Energy Data Base* of the Department of Energy.

- Some 2,000 federal machine-readable statistical data files will be

cataloged and indexed in cooperation with the Office of Federal
Statistical Policy and Standards.

• A current computer software catalog has been published.

• Extensive efforts are being made to expand the present NTIS collection of machine-readable data files and software programs.

Another new emphasis for NTIS concerns the unilateral outflow of
U.S. technical information to foreign countries. Ours is a free and open
democratic society and, as a matter of national policy, Americans share
their scientific and technical information in the hope that its application
will help improve the quality of life for all mankind.

Americans encourage the full international exchange of scientific and
technical information. While it is true that there has been some inflow of
foreign information, usually through the scientific journals, it has been
disappointingly small and, for a great many areas of technology, nonexistent. There are many reasons why technological information is not
flowing into the United States. We must acknowledge that for many
years U.S. business and industry were not particularly interested in
knowing about or using foreign technology. This parochial attitude has
changed more and more as foreign products have claimed an ever-
increasing and, in some cases, dominant share of the U.S. market. At
the same time, U.S. products have not fared very well in foreign markets. Industry is now becoming increasingly interested in foreign technology, and the NTIS program fully intends to respond to this need.

The NTIS program provides for the *extensive* inclusion of foreign technical literature and translations in order to make the relevant information available to business and industry. This goal will be accomplished
by locating, acquiring, and announcing to U.S. industry selected foreign
technical literature. An added feature will be translations of the most
important items, thus making them more widely and easily available.

Now let us turn quickly and briefly to another major program that
provides some real incentives to the entrepreneur—*Government Inventions and Patents for Licensing*.

This program encompasses three areas: announcement and promotion of all government-owned inventions; evaluation and selection of
commercially promising inventions; and highly selective filing for protection of foreign rights.

The government produces approximately 1,300 inventions each year,
for which various agencies file applications with the U.S. Patent and
Trademark Office. These agencies then send to NTIS copies of the patent applications and the patents themselves for processing and announce-

ment to the public. The patent applications and patents are catalogued and indexed, and all pertinent data, including abstracts, are entered into the NTIS data base.

Worthy of note here is the six-volume *Catalog of Government Patents* that contains information on more than 20,000 government-owned inventions dating back to 1966. Updates are issued annually. NTIS feels that a patent, because of the strict requirements on it for novelty and utility, has far greater potential for stimulating industrial innovation than the average technical report, provided it is packaged and marketed with this objective in mind.

In the early 1970s, the Committee on Government Patent Policy highlighted the need for greater exploitation of government-owned patents to foster the domestic economy. It asked NTIS to act as the central nexus for the publication of information on all government-owned inventions. Announcements of patent applications in the *Federal Register* were started in 1972 and in the *Official Gazette* in 1973. The weekly abstract newsletter, "Government Inventions for Licensing," was launched the same year.

The Committee on Government Patent Policy recommended that NTIS supplement the publication of abstracts and notices of license availability with publicity by means of technical briefs and direct solicitation. These programs were started in 1976 by the Office of Government Inventions and Patents, established by NTIS the year before. Also in 1976, "memoranda of understanding" were signed with the Department of Agriculture, the Department of Interior, the Department of Health and Human Services, and the Department of Transportation to transfer to the Secretary of Commerce the foreign rights to inventions considered by NTIS to have commercial and technical potential.

In 1977 an inventor's incentive award system was inaugurated under memoranda of understanding, thus permitting a minor percentage of the annual royalties from licensed inventions to flow back to the inventors.

The overall NTIS patent program encompasses invention evaluation, foreign filing, invention promotion, and use of patent licensing by U.S. industry for technical innovation. A number of royalty-bearing licenses have been granted. As with all new programs and with innovation itself, there will be an latency period of a number of years before a steady flow of new agreements and royalties will develop, enabling the program to recover its start-up costs. It is anticipated that the program will be self-sustaining in several years and will thereafter exert a significant effect on domestic technical innovation and on U.S. international trade relations.

Before closing, I would like to share with you NTIS's long-term goals for the 1980s. Briefly stated, they are to

- convert NTIS from a labor-intensive to a technology-intensive organization through the application of advanced information processing and dissemination technologies;

- convert NTIS from a "document organization" to an "information organization" by developing prototype products;

- develop new and improved information products for U.S. business and industry, with particular emphasis on products targeted for use by front-line engineers and technicians;

- improve coordination with other Department of Commerce agencies on technical information dissemination;

- acquire, process, and disseminate more information on foreign technology by adding new sources each year; and

- achieve self-supporting status for all NTIS programs.

As you can see, many exciting things are happening at NTIS. We are looking forward to taking these important steps to help meet the nation's commitment to improved productivity and innovation and the continuing challenge to maintain the technological strength of the American economy.

FREEDOM OF INFORMATION IN CANADA AT THE FEDERAL LEVEL*

By R. Brian Land

Introduction

In dealing with Freedom of Information legislation in Canada, this chapter shall attempt, wherever possible, to make reference to the U.S. Freedom of Information Act[1] in order to provide the reader with a point of reference. But before discussing the Freedom of Information legislation currently before the Canadian Parliament, it should be mentioned that, whereas in the United States the executive and legislative arms of government are separate, in Canada the executive is drawn from the legislature and the prime minister and members of his Cabinet sit in the House of Commons.[2] This difference becomes significant when comparing the application of the two pieces of legislation, particularly with regard to the procedures for an appeal to the courts in the event of a denial of information access. Another important distinction is that, unlike members of Congress, who may call for and see any and all documents they seek, Canadian members of Parliament have no right of access to certain exempted categories of information.

---

*The author would like to acknowledge the assistance in preparing this paper of Philip Kaye, Research Officer, Ontario Legislative Library, Research and Information Services.

Historical Background

The issue of freedom of information has been the subject of public attention in Canada for more than fifteen years. The first Freedom of Information bill was introduced in Parliament in 1965 as a private member's bill by a member of the New Democratic Party.[3] In 1969, a federal Task Force on Government Information published a report titled *To Know and Be Known*, asserting that a new information policy should rest on the twin principles that "the Government has an obligation to provide full, objective and timely information; and that the citizens have a right to such information."[4] The Task Force described the U.S. Freedom of Information Act as a "major legislative achievement," but pointed out that at that time (1969) comparatively little use was being made of it.[5]

Notices of Motion for the Production of Papers

In February 1973, the Cabinet issued a directive entitled "Notices of Motion for the Production of Papers."[6] This directive identified the kinds of government records that could be produced for members of Parliament. It affirmed the need "to make public as much factual information as possible, consistent with effective administration, the protection of the security of the state, rights to privacy and other such matters."[7] Despite this affirmation, most of the document consists of sixteen criteria, any one of which, if satisfied, would exempt the government from production of papers. In the absence of Freedom of Information legislation, these guidelines are still in effect.

Bill C-225

It was not until 1974 that freedom of information received serious attention from Canadian parliamentarians. In that year, Gerald Baldwin, a Progressive Conservative M.P., introduced Bill C-225 dealing with the Public's right to know the public business.[8] His bill, along with the Cabinet directive previously mentioned, were referred to the Standing Joint Committee on Regulations and Other Statutory Instruments. After holding numerous public hearings in 1974 and 1975, the committee tabled in Parliament its report containing an endorsement of the principle of Freedom of Information. The report was approved unanimously by the House in February 1976, marking the first parliamentary step toward the introduction of Freedom of Information legislation at the federal level in Canada.[9]

The Green Paper

The next notable event in the progression toward the goal of freedom of information was the publication by the Department of the Secretary of State of a "Green Paper," a proposal for "Legislation on Public Access to Government Documents."[10] Although the Green Paper supported the principle of open access (subject to specified exemptions), a recurring theme was the need to preserve ministerial control over access to information and opposition to independent review of ministerial decisions to withhold information. The Green Paper was referred to the Standing Joint Committee on Regulations and Other Statutory Instruments in December 1977. After conducting extensive hearings, the committee tabled its report in Parliament in June 1978, recommending the adoption of tough Freedom of Information legislation.[11]

Introduction of Bill C-15

In October 1979, pursuant to its campaign promises, the new Progressive Conservative Government introduced Bill C-15, The Freedom of Information Act, in the House of Commons.[12] In general terms, Bill C-15 opted for a Freedom of Information scheme based on the U.S. model, recognizing a general right of access (again subject to certain exemptions). A mediation process would have allowed a so-called Information Commissioner to review documents and to recommend, but not order, their disclosure. Ultimate appeal was to be to the Federal Court, which would determine whether or not an exemption applied to the record in dispute. The Federal Court's *de novo* review jurisdiction resembled that of the district courts under the U.S. Act. Bill C-15 had barely reached the committee stage when the government of Prime Minister Joe Clark was defeated in the House of Commons, an election was called, and Pierre Trudeau and the Liberal Party were returned to power.

Bill C-43

On July 17, 1980, Bill C-43, legislation to implement the Access to Information Act and the Privacy Act, to amend the Federal Court Act and the Canada Evidence Act, and to amend certain other acts in consequence thereof, was introduced in the House of Commons by the Liberal Government and given a first reading.[13] The Access to Information part of the bill consists of thirty-seven pages plus a nine-page schedule of government institutions to which the bill applies. This is in sharp contrast to the four-page U.S. Freedom of Information Act. On January 29, 1981, Bill C-43 received a second reading and was referred to the Standing

Committee on Justice and Legal Affairs for study and report. The committee has passed several amendments to the bill but has not yet completed its deliberations.

Overview of the Bill

Right of Access to Information

As mentioned, Bill C-43 has both Freedom of Information and privacy components. The central principle of the Access to Information Act (which constitutes Schedule 1 of the bill) is "that government information should be available to the public, that necessary exceptions to the right of access should be limited and specific, and that decisions on the disclosure of government information should be reviewed independently of government" (s.2). Similarly, the U.S. Freedom of Information Act provides that "any person" is entitled to see agency records unless the record in question falls under an exemption [subss. (a) (3) and (b)].

The second part of Bill C-43, the Privacy Act, confers a right of access to personal information in government files concerning the requester. While Part IV of the Canadian Human Rights Act[14] currently limits that right to information found in administrative data banks, Bill C-43 extends access to any other personal data concerning the individual which is reasonably retrievable [Schedule II, s.12 (1) (b)]. For purposes of this presentation, attention will be focused on the Access to Information Act as amended to date in committee.

Scope

The proposed legislation applies to "Government Institutions," which are defined as "any department or ministry of state of the Government of Canada listed in the schedule" accompanying the Bill (s.3). Thus, unless an institution appears in the list of 28 departments and 102 agencies, it is excluded from the scope of the Act. The exclusion of certain commercial Crown corporations, such as Air Canada, the government-owned airline, has been justified on the grounds that their competitive position in the marketplace must be protected.[15] The U.S. Act follows a different approach, applying as it does to each federal agency, including state-owned or -controlled corporations. Nor does the U.S. Act provide for specific exemptions tailored to the commercial activities of such bodies.[16]

Exemptions

One of the most controversial sections of Bill C-43 relates to exemptions. Sixteen sections of the bill create exemptions from the general right of access. Information that can be withheld by heads of government institutions includes:

- Information obtained in confidence from foreign, provincial, or municipal governments, or international organizations, unless the submitter of the information consents to disclosure or makes the information public (s.13).

- Information whose disclosure could affect adversely federal-provincial negotiations (s.14).

- Information whose release might cause injury to the conduct of international affairs, defenses, or counterintelligence (s.15).

- Information relating to law enforcement and criminal investigations (s.16).

- Information whose disclosure could threaten the safety of individuals (s.17).

- Information whose release could reasonably be expected to be materially injurious to the financial interests of the Canadian government or to its ability to manage the Canadian economy (s.18).

- Personal information, unless: the individual to whom it relates consents to the disclosure; the information is publicly available; or the public interest in disclosure clearly outweighs any resultant invasion of privacy (s.19).

- Third party information, such as trade secrets and confidential information, unless the third party consents to disclosure (s.20).

- Memoranda to Cabinet, discussion papers and other Cabinet documents, although discussion papers may be released after decisions of Cabinet are made public (s.21).

- Advice and accounts of consultations involving Ministers and staff (s.22).

- Information relating to testing or auditing procedures if disclosure prejudices the use or results of tests or audits (s.23).

- Information subject to solicitor-client privilege (s.24).

- Information whose disclosure is restricted by other statutes (s.25).

- Material that will be published within 90 days after a request or within a further period, if needed for printing or translation (s.27).

- Records in existence more than five years before the coming into force of the Act (can be withheld for up to three years) (s.28).

- Published material, library or museum material preserved solely for reference or exhibition purposes, or material placed in the Public Archives other than by government institutions (s.67).

Exemptions Compared

A detailed comparison between this extensive list and the nine exemptions in the U.S. Act is beyond the scope of this chapter. In general, however, the Canadian provisions are unique to the extent that they comprise both permissive and mandatory exemptions. The U.S. statute permits agencies to withhold certain kinds of documents, but they are not required to do so. Thus, agencies retain a discretion to disclose information that is technically exempt.[17] On the other hand, some of the exemptions in C-43 begin, "The head of a government institution *shall* [emphasis added] refuse to disclose...." Unless disclosure is specifically authorized, there is no discretion whatsoever to release documents. The exemptions which fall into this category pertain to confidential information received from other governments [s. 13 (1)], personal privacy [s. 19 (1)], commercial information [s. 20 (1)], cabinet records [s. 21 (1) and (2)], and other statutory prohibitions [s. 25 (1)].[18] The factors that determine whether an exemption will be permissive or mandatory are unclear.

From a comparative perspective, a Canadian law professor, John McCamus, has criticized the exemptions in C-43 as being too broad. He writes:

Those which touch on the same subject areas as those in the American Act—policy-making, national security, law enforcement, commercial information and personal privacy—are invariably more protective of government confidentiality than are the exemptions pertaining to these matters in the American scheme. Further, C-43 adds a significant number of exemptions which have no equivalent in the American Act and which appear to be either unnecessary or too restrictive in their design.[19]

Section 16 (1) (a) of the Canadian Bill, for example, gives the Cabinet power to exempt by order-in-council virtually all investigative records less than twenty years old that are held by a law enforcement agency.[20] There is no similar provision in the U.S. Act, although, since McCamus wrote his analysis, efforts have continued in the Congress to amend the Act in order to allow the Attorney General to exempt all records relating to terrorism, organized crime and counterintelligence investigations.[21]

Both the proposed Canadian legislation and the U.S. Freedom of Information Act adopt the principle of severability. Thus, if a requested record contains both exempt and non-exempt material, reasonable efforts must be made to sever and disclose the non-exempt portion [C-43, s. 26; 5 U.S.C. 552 (b)].

Appeal and Review Procedures

Bill C-43 provides for a two-stage appeal and review procedure for complaints from persons who have been refused access to a record. There is provision for an initial appeal to an Information Commissioner, which may be followed by an appeal to the Federal Court of Canada. If the Information Commissioner finds that the complaint is well-founded, a report is directed to the head of the government institution in question. The report will include the findings of the commissioner's investigation and any recommendations that are to be considered appropriate. The recommendations do not bind the institution but, if access is still denied, the complainant can appeal to the Federal Court (ss. 31, 38 and 42).

The jurisdiction of the Federal Court represents a compromise between the principles of ministerial responsibility and judicial review. For the most part, the court can conduct a full *de novo* review and reach its own determination on the applicability of an exemption. But with respect to four exemptions, namely federal-provincial affairs (s. 14), international affairs and defense (s. 15), law enforcement [s. 16 (c)], and the economic interests of Canada [s. 18 (c)], the court's appellate jurisdiction is restricted. It can only order disclosure if the head of the institution did not have "reasonable grounds" to invoke the exemption (ss. 50 and 51).[22]

These qualifications on judicial power are derived from the concept of ministerial responsibility. Ministers are accountable for their decisions to Parliament and to the public. According to the Green Paper of 1977, if judges could replace ministerial decisions with their own opinions, they would be changing their role entirely and entering the political arena.[23] Moreover, the Green Paper asserted that "there is no way that a judicial officer can be properly made aware of all the political, economic, social and security factors that may have led to the decision in issue."[24] It appears that the government views these factors as especially relevant when applying the four exemptions cited above.

One of the features of Bill C-43 is that third parties (that is, persons or organizations other than the requester) are granted appeal rights. First of all, they must be notified when information that could adversely affect their interests is to be released. Then, they are allowed to make representations opposing disclosure and may appeal to the Federal Court a decision to release the information (ss. 29 and 45).

Under the U.S. Act, a requester can appeal "any adverse determination" to the head of the agency [subs. (a) (6) (A) (i)]. Further appeal must be to the district court, which can order release if the document is not covered by an exemption. Third parties are not given any rights of appeal.

Unlike the Federal Court of Canada, the U.S. District Court can always determine the matter *de novo* [subs. (a) (4) (B)]. In the proceedings before both courts, the burden of proof is on the government to sustain its action, and a judge is entitled to examine the record in dispute [C-43, ss. 47 and 49; 5 U.S.C. 552 (a) (4) (B)].

Exercising the Right of Access

Definition of "Record"

Rights of access under both the Canadian and American legislation extend to "records," but only Bill C-43 defines this term. Bill C-43 includes a broad definition of "record" to include "any correspondence, memorandum, book, plan, map, drawing, diagram, pictorial or graphic work, photograph, film, microfilm, sound recording, videotape, machine-readable record, and any other documentary material, regardless of physical form or characteristics, and any copy thereof." (s. 3).

The word "record" has also been broadly interpreted in the U.S. legislation. It is not restricted to a piece of paper, but includes any tangible record of information in any form whatsoever. Recently, however, there has been some litigation over the issue of what constitutes an *agency* [emphasis added] record. Mere possession by an agency may not be sufficient for asserting a right of access to a document.[25]

Limitations on the Right of Access

As originally drafted, Bill C-43 would have limited the right of access to records to Canadian citizens, permanent residents, and Canadian corporations. In contrast, "any person," anywhere in the world, can invoke the American Freedom of Information Act. [subs. (a) (3)]. An amendment to C-43 by the Committee on Justice and Legal Affairs would allow the Cabinet to extend the right of access to persons other than Canadian citizens and permanent residents. The intent of the amendment is to empower the Cabinet to permit the right of access to residents of countries which have reciprocal arrangements. Foreigners, then do not have an automatic right of access; a Cabinet order would have to be issued first.[26]

Identification of Records

Under Bill C-43, requests for information must provide "sufficient detail to enable an experienced employee of the institution with a reasonable effort to identify the record." (s. 6). The American statute requires individuals to reasonably describe the records in question. [subs. (a) (3)]. The interpretation of this requirement resembles that of the Canadian provision. The Deputy Director of the Office of Information Law and Policy of the U.S. Department of Justice in Washington has explained that "the request must be sufficiently specific to enable a professional employee who is familiar with the agency's records to understand what is being requested and to locate it with reasonable effort."[27]

Publications about Government Institutions

In order to facilitate the identification of records by requesters, indexes are essential. Section 5 of Bill C-43 provides for the issuance of "a publication" at least once a year and an updating "bulletin" at least twice each year. The "publication" must contain "a description of the organization and responsibilities of each government institution" and "the title and address of the appropriate officer for each government institution to whom requests for access to records...should be sent" [s. 5 (1) (a) and (d)]. In addition, there must be "a description of all classes of records under the control of each government institution" [s. 5 (1) (b)].

As initially drafted, Bill C-43 allowed exempt material to be excluded from listing in the "publication" or "bulletin" [s. 5 (3)]. The Canadian Library Association objected that members of the general public would have no way of knowing about the existence of material judged to be exempt and would therefore be unable to ask for its disclosure or to appeal its exemption to the Information Commissioner.[28] As amended, the subsection provides that all classes of records must be described, even if they are exemptable.

The "publication" must also contain "a description of all manuals used by employees of each government institution in administering or carrying out any of the programs or activities of the government institution" [s.5 (1) (c)]. The manuals themselves, though, do not have to be made accessible to the public. However, the government subsequently tabled an amendment which would require the head of every government institution to provide, within two years after the section comes into force, facilities where the public may inspect any manual used by employees.[30]

Another amendment to C-43 gives the Information Commissioner specific power to investigate complaints in respect of the "publication" or "bulletin."[31] The findings would then be reported to Parliament (s.39).

The U.S. Act also provides for a register and index of government information. Each agency must publish in the *Federal Register* several categories of information, ranging from a description of its organization to its rules of procedure [subs. (a) (1)]. This requirement is designed to ensure that the guidelines followed by an agency in its dealings with the public are published.[32] Furthermore, each agency must make available for public inspection and copying (a) final opinions and orders, (b) statements of policy and interpretations, and (c) administrative staff manuals and instructions to staff that affect a member of the public. Current indexes of these records must be made available to the public [Subs. (a) (2)].

Time Limits

The Canadian and American acts differ significantly in the amount of time allocated for responding to requests. Under C-43, the head of the institution must, within thirty days, notify the requester as to whether access will be given or denied and, if the former, grant access to the record (s.7). Failure to respond is deemed a refusal of access [s.10 (3)]. The government may extend the time limit for an undefined "reasonable period" where the records are voluminous and compliance with the thirty-day period "would unreasonably interfere with the operations of the government institution" [s.9 (1) (a)]. Extensions are also permissible if consultations are necessary or if third parties must be given notice of the request (commercial records) [s.9 (1) (b) and (c)]. If access is denied, a complaint may be filed with the Information Commissioner up to one year after the Government first received the request (s. 32). After the Commissioner reports the results of an investigation to the complainant, there is a minimum of forty-five days within which to appeal to the federal court (s. 42).

The American Act sets a much shorter limit of ten working days for an initial response to a request. If an appeal is taken, an agency must make a ruling within twenty working days (subs. (a) (6) (A)). The statute authorizes in "unusual circumstances" (subs. (a) (6) (B)) an extension of these limits by a combined total of ten working days (s. 10). If the

Agency does not respond within the requisite time period, the requester can apply immediately for judicial review [subs. (a) (6) (c)].

Existence of Records

The Canadian Bill permits the head of the government institution to refuse access without indicating whether or not the record exists. The requester, though, is notified of the provision under which an exemption would be claimed if the record did in fact exist (s. 10). The American Act does not confer any similar power on federal agencies. In the view of some investigatory agencies, this kind of clause can prevent individuals who pose significant security or law enforcement risks from discovering if they are the subject of an investigation.[33]

Fees and Copies

Bill C-43, as amended, states that "a person who makes a request for access to a record under this act may be required to pay" an application fee not exceeding $25.00 [(s.11 (1) (a)]. A further payment may be demanded "for every hour in excess of five hours that is reasonably required to search for the record or prepare any part of it for disclosure" [s.11 (2)]. Although the head of the government institution may waive the fee or provide a refund, no guidelines are stipulated for the exercise of this discretion [s. 11 (6)].

Another amendment by the Committee on Justice and Legal Affairs holds that a person who is given access to a record can, subject to the regulations, examine the record or obtain a copy [s.12 (1)].

Bill C-43 authorizes the charging of reproduction costs to the requester [s. 11 (1) (b)]. A copy of a record must be provided in either official language (English or French), if so requested and if a translation is considered to be in the public interest [s. 12 (2) (b)]. Another provision clarifies that the making of copies does not constitute an infringement of the copyright laws [subs.12 (3) and (4)].[34]

The U.S. Act limits fees to the direct costs of search and duplication. Consequently, agencies cannot charge for time spent reviewing records to determine whether they are exempt. A similar charge is prohibited under the Canadian bill. The U.S. Act requires that documents must be supplied free of charge or at a reduced charge "where the agency determines that waiver or reduction of the fee is in the public interest because furnishing the information can be considered as primarily benefiting the general public" [subs. (a) (4) (A)]. As mentioned previously, criteria for the waiving of fees are absent from C-43.

Conclusion

Canadian and American experience confirms that Freedom of Information acts are not legislated quickly. The passage of Bill C-43 has been stalled in committee because of objections from provincial attorneys general. The provinces are especially concerned about three issues: (1) the abolition of absolute Crown privilege, (2) the protection of sensitive law enforcement information, and (3) the existence of an appeal procedure that gives the courts, rather than politicians, the final say on disclosure. The Ontario Attorney-General has recently suggested that the federal government drop attempts to pass Bill C-43 and instead draft, with provincial involvement, a uniform Freedom of Information statute covering all governments. As a consequence of these provincial interventions, the Cabinet has instructed the minister responsible for Bill C-43 to consider the provincial objections and prepare a report before proceeding with the bill.[35]

As a result, there is little or no chance that Bill C-43 will be out of committee before the present session of Parliament is prorogued. The government is now faced with three choices: first, to reintroduce the bill at the next session of Parliament in much the same form as at present; second, to water down the bill in response to pressure from the provinces; and third, to withdraw the bill completely.

The chances of passage of federal Freedom of Information legislation in Canada, which only four months ago looked excellent, now appear to have diminished considerably. Advocates of Bill C-43 can only hope that the government's initial resolution to provide Canadians with the legal right of access to government information will prevail. If so, Canada would become the first national government in the Commonwealth to have a freedom of information act.

References

1. *Freedom of Information Act*, 5 U.S. Code 552 (1966).

2. During the first session of the 32nd Parliament, four Senators have been members of the Cabinet. The normal practice in recent years has been to have one Senator only, namely, the Leader of the Government in the Senate, as a member of the Cabinet, reflecting the fact that the Canadian Senate is not an elected but an appointed body.

3. Canada. Laws, statutes, etc. Bills of the House of Commons. *Bill C-39, An Act to Better Assure the Public's Right to Freedom of Access to Public Documents and Information about Government Administration (Administrative Disclosure)*. Barry Mather. 1st reading, 8 April 1965.

4. Canada. Task Force on Government Information. *To Know and Be Known: Report*. (Ottawa: Queen's Printer, 1969.) 1:49.

5. Ibid., 2:28.

6. Canada. Cabinet. *Directive Number 45: Notices of Motion for the Production of Papers*. (Ottawa, 1973.)

7. Ibid., p. 1

8. Canada. Laws, statutes, etc. Bills of the House of Commons. *Bill C-225, An Act Representing the Right of the Public to Information Concerning the Public Business*. Gerald W. Baldwin. 1st reading, 15 October 1974.

9. Canada. Parliament. House of Commons. *Journals*. 30th Parliament. 1st session. 12 February 1976, p. 1016.

10. Canada. Dept. of the Secretary of State. *Legislation on Public Access to Government Documents*. (Ottawa: Supply and Services Canada, 1977).

11. Canada. Parliament. House of Commons. Standing Joint Committee on Regulations and other Statutory Instruments. *Fifth Report. Journals*. 30th Parliament, 3rd session. 28 June 1978, pp. 916-925.

12. Canada. Laws, statutes, etc. Bills of the House of Commons. *Bill C-15, An Act to Extend the Present Laws of Canada that Provide Access to Information Under the Control of the Government of Canada and to Amend the Canada Evidence Act, the Federal Court Act and the Statutory Instruments Act*. The Hon. Walter Baker. 1st reading, 24 October 1979.

13. Canada. Laws, statutes, etc. Bills of the House of Commons. *Bill C-43, An Act to Enact the Access to Information Act and the Privacy Act, to Amend the Federal Court Act and the Canada Evidence Act, and to Amend Certain Other Acts in Consequence Thereof*. The Hon. Francis Fox. 1st reading, 17 July 1980.

14. Canada. Laws, statutes, etc. *Canadian Human Rights Act*. (Ottawa, 1977.)

15. Canada. Parliament. House of Commons. Standing Committee on Justice and Legal Affairs. *Minutes of Proceedings and Evidence*. 32nd Parliament. 1st session. No. 37, 2 June 1981. (Ottawa, 1981), pp. 13-14.

16. *See* John D. McCamus, "Bill C-43: The Federal Canadian Proposals of 1980," in *Freedom of Information: Canadian Perspectives*, ed. John D. McCamus (Toronto: Butterworths, 1981), p. 269.

17. Douglas S. Wood, "The American Freedom of Information Act," in *Freedom of Information: Canadian Perspectives*, p. 199.

18. Another mandatory exemption was added by the Justice Committee when the words "may refuse" were replaced by "shall refuse" in subs. 16(3). The subsection applies to information obtained by the Royal Canadian Mounted Police while performing services for provinces or municipalities. *Proceedings*, no. 46, June 26, 1981, pp. 14-15.

19. McCamus, "Bill C-43: The Federal Canadian Proposals of 1980," p. 279.

20. Ibid., p. 287. The twenty year qualification was added by the Justice Committee.

21. U.S., Congress, Senate, *Freedom of Information Reform Act*, S. 1730, 97th Cong., 1st sess., 1981, s. 11(a). On 14 December 1981, this bill was approved with amendments by the Judiciary Constitution Subcommittee.

22. The Justice Committee relettered s. 18(c) as s. 18(d). *Proceedings*, no. 47, 30 June 1981, pp. 28-30. It is assumed that s. 51's reference to s. 18(c) will be amended accordingly.

23. *Legislation on Public Access*, p. 17.

24. Ibid., p. 18.

25. Wood, "The American Freedom of Information Act," p. 196.

26. *Proceedings*, no. 38, 4 June 1981, pp. 25-26; no. 39, 9 June 1981, p. 15.

27. Wood, "The American Freedom of Information Act," p. 197.

28. *Proceedings*, no. 21, 24 March 1981. *Canadian Library Association. Brief.* App. "JLA-10", p. 21.

29. *Proceedings*, no. 39, 9 June 1981, p. 36.

30. Ibid., no. 40, 11 June 1981, p. 25. The amendment will appear as s. 69(1).

31. Ibid., no. 54, 19 November 1981, p. 17. A paragraph is added to s. 31.

32. Wood, "The American Freedom of Information Act," p. 195.

33. McCamus, "Bill C-43: The Federal Canadian Proposals of 1980," p. 272; Tom Riley, "A Comparison of Information Laws in the U.S. and Canada," *Journal of Media Law and Practice* 2 (September 1981): 192.

34. *Proceedings*, no. 42, 17 June 1981, p. 8 Subss. 12(3) and (4) of C-43 have been replaced by proposed amendments to the *Copyright Act*. These amendments will be added to Schedule IV of Bill C-43 ("Consequential Amendments").

35. *Globe and Mail* (Toronto), 11 December 1981; 3 February 1982; 12 February 1982.

GOVERNMENT-PRODUCED MACHINE-READABLE STATISTICAL DATA AS A COMPONENT OF THE SOCIAL SCIENCE INFORMATION SYSTEM: AN EXAMINATION OF FEDERAL POLICY AND STRATEGIES FOR ACCESS

By Kathleen M. Heim

Introduction

Library and information center facilitation of public use of machine-readable, numeric governmental data presents problems fraught with many complexities. To describe methods by which the "public" may acquire and use these data requires an understanding of the diversity of that public, as well as a general characterization of these data and the kinds of use to which they might be put.

In the largest sense the "public" needing government-produced statistical data may be any individual, institution, or business requiring information for decision-making. For many needs, the printed material issued by the government is sufficient; for the needs of more sophisticated information users, access to government statistics in machine-readable formats to facilitate complex computer analyses may be required. Since we do not attempt here to address the total statistical information requirements of the nation, we will define as our public the social scientist, usually affiliated with an academic institution, who requires social science data in machine-readable form to investigate social problems, either to make recommendations for public policy or to examine issues for general understanding. The reasons why social scientists require governmental data vary with their discipline. The difficulty in defining the areas of social science concern described in the first major portion of this chapter also creates problems in developing information responses to meet social scientific needs.

Strategies for developing access to government statistical data are the focus of the second portion of this chapter, which summarizes libraries' failure to provide machine-readable data, current Federal access policies, and means by which documents librarians might facilitate access in the future.

The range of data we are discussing is enormous. It includes such machine-readable numeric files as: the CIA's *World Data Bank II*—geographic reference files; the USDA's *Crops Official Estimates*—time series summary statistics containing crop estimates by commodity for the U.S. by state from 1954 to the present; the Department of Commerce's *Census of Population and Housing, 1970 Educational Attainment Summary Statistics* —records for geographic areas containing data on years of school completed cross-classified by a variety of demographic characteristics for the total and Black populations; the Department of Education's *National Assessment of Educational Progress*—summary statistics corresponding to communities on educational achievement for selected groups by data including parental education with response ranges to tests on math, science, social studies, music, reading and literature; the Department of Health and Human Services' *Vital Statistics, Divorce*; the Social Security Administration's *Continuous Work History Sample*; the Bureau of Justice Statistics' *National Crime Survey*; the FBI's *Uniform Crime Reports*; or the Bureau of Labor Statistics' *LABSTAT*—100,000 economic time series data pertaining to the labor force and other parts of the economy.

Once acquired by social scientists, such statistics enable an analysis of evaluative and policy-relevant data to be made, usually in ways other than those used in the original analysis.[1] Boruch, Cordray and Wortman explain the rationale for secondary analysis of these kinds of data in their recent book, *Reanalyzing Program Evaluations*. The general justification includes the need to assess programs of the government as to effectiveness; the verification of the quality of information and analysis; the re-using of expensive data sets for several purposes; and meta-analysis— the reviewing of the results of different studies and the combining of statistical estimates of program effects to obtain a composite view of the effect of planned interventions.[2]

Since machine-readable statistical data are growing in importance as a social science resource, it is important to try to understand the infrastructure of the social science information system in order to place this resource in a framework from which to develop information services that take this framework into consideration. To do this this chapter will first describe what is understood about the social science information system as a whole and then proceed to explore the development of response mechanisms for machine-readable statistical information provision, with a focus on government produced data.

PART I: THE SOCIAL SCIENCE INFORMATION SYSTEM

The Scope of the Social Sciences and Their Information Needs

Although access to information in the social sciences is available through a variety of publications, libraries, information services and data banks, these services are still largely uncoordinated.[3] J. M. Brittain, a frequent commentator on the state of social science information, has noted that the planning and development of new services, and the coordination and rationalization of existing ones, requires, first of all, a knowledge of the current state of affairs, which means details about the number, range, and type of services for each major subject, language, and country.[4]

The perplexing problem of even conclusively *defining* the social sciences has been difficult for information providers. Major organizers of the literature of social science research have approached the problem in a variety of ways. Carl M. White, whose volume, *Sources of Information in the Social Sciences*, acts as a primary organizer notes:

The literature of the social sciences covers eight fields that have, in common a concern for the behavior of man in relation to his fellows and to the environment they share. Foremost among them, for tested knowledge, are sociology, psychology, anthropology, economics, and political science. Geography overlaps these subjects but has its own contributions to make on interactions between man and the land. Education is more an art than a science, but is included because it draws so extensively on these other disciplines and because of its own research. History has close ties with the humanities. They are concerned the same as the social science with man, his ways, and works, but normally rely on different methods—critical analysis, creative imagination, and the arts of expression and persuasion. For a century and more, however, historians have been perfecting methods of objective inquiry, thereby establishing inseparable connections with the social sciences. Perhaps establishing inseparable connections with the methods from the two great scholarly traditions, the humanistic and the empirical.

A case can be made for including still other subjects, from statistics to journalism and law, but we have to stop somewhere and this is a convenient place. Specialists in these eight fields bear most of the responsibility for developing interconnected, empirically based propositions about human behavior and its social consequences. They tend to draw on one another's work; and the total literature, while bulky and growing, can be surveyed in a single volume of manageable size.[5]

Bert F. Hoselitz's *A Reader's Guide to the Social Sciences* includes only six disciplines: sociology, anthropology, psychology, political science, economics, and geography—leaving out education and history.[6] Thelma Freides in her *Literature and Bibliography of the Social Sciences* states, "The disciplines customarily designated 'social sciences' are psychology, anthropology, political science, sociology, economics, geography, and history."[7] She thus concurs with Hoselitz's omission of education, but acknowledges the fuzzy limits of the social sciences by noting:

There is no single way to define or enumerate the social sciences. Very generally, they are the fields whose interest centers on observation and explanation of the actions of people in society: what people do and why, and under what circumstances they do one thing rather than another. The most general custom is to designate as social sciences the *seven* disciplines enumerated above.[8]

Foskett, whose work in the classification of the social sciences has also compelled him to consider the question, breaks down all fields of knowledge into the natural sciences (the study of objects and processes in the universe irrespective of man); humanities (the study of the intellectual productions of man); and the social sciences (the study of man and his relations with other men)—anthropology, sociology, political science, law, economics, history, geography, psychology, and education.[9]

Table 4-1 provides a comparison of the various disciplines for inclusion in the social sciences as identified by the major organizers of social science information: White, Hoselitz, Foskett, and Freides.

The problem of defining the social sciences has been noted in order to underscore the problem of providing information to them. The types of material that must come under archival and bibliographic control to serve these varied disciplines are enormous. In his classic work on the subject, *The Tools of Social Science*, John Madge enumerated the range of materials of use to researchers in these disciplines:

(1) personal documents, including letters, folklore, life histories, autobiographies, diaries and letters; (2) records, including records of professional societies, committee records, government reports; (3) reports that are made after an event, e.g. newspaper reports; (4) observations, including mass observation where the investigator may penetrate into the environment he is observing; (5) data from "action research" where the investigator resides in the target area for a period to observe the group life, morale, and productivity of a single community with the aim of developing effective ways of resolving social stress and tension and facilitating agreed and desired social change; (6) "overheard" data from passive observation; (7) data from interviews such as Gallup polls, opinion polls, scalogram analyses, and measures of attitude; (8) data from experiments, usually conducted in controlled environments in laboratories.[10]

**Table 4-1: Disciplines Identified as Belonging to the Social Sciences
by Major Organizers of Social Science Information**

Disciplines	Major Organizers			
	White*	Hoselitz*	Freides*	Foskett*
Sociology	X	X	X	X
Psychology	X	X	X	X
Anthropology	X	X	X	X
Economics	X	X	X	X
Political Science	X	X	X	X
Geography	X	X	X	X
Education	X			X
History	X		X	X
Law			X	X

*Sources: Carl M. White et al., *Sources of Information in the Social Sciences: A
Guide to the Literature*, 2nd ed. (Chicago: American Library Association,
1973); Bert F. Hoselitz, ed. *A Reader's Guide to the Social Sciences*, rev.
ed. (New York: The Free Press, 1970); Thelma Freides, *Literature and
Bibliography of the Social Sciences* (Los Angeles: Melville Publishing,
1973); D. J. Foskett, *Classification and Indexing in the Social Sciences*
(London: Butterworths, 1974).

Madge's item seven was emphasized in a 1967 U.S. National Research
Council report on communication in the behavioral sciences, which noted
that "at least as pressing a problem as the management of digested
information, or the *output* of research, is the development of raw data
resources as the *input* for research."[11] These needs range from the simu-
lations of mass political opinion formulation based on large assemblages
of survey data to modeling data. As the quantitative approach spreads
throughout the behavioral sciences, requirements for control over these
kinds of information will become more pressing. The report strongly

emphasized that while conventional documentation problems in the social sciences deserve attention, "those relating to the organization of data resources in a broader sense are more significant for the future, for they reflect new and relatively unfamiliar needs, have fewer counterparts in the physical sciences, and directly touch issues associated with national informational and administrative requirements."[12] Documentation and organization of social science information continues to be a difficult problem. The next section will survey attempts to articulate the structure of systemic response to social science information requirements.

Attempts to Develop Models of the Social Science Information System

What kind of information system serves the social science disciplines? The 1950 Chicago study, "Bibliographical Services in the Social Sciences," found bibliographical services for the social sciences unsatisfactory. While an array of various services provided at least partial coverage of books, journal articles, government documents, and dissertations, *sources of data* (as distinguished from scholarly publications) were seen as so diverse that it was found impossible to attempt to index them.[13] Thus, early on we find established the dichotomy between two major types of materials of social science research: data and scholarly publications.

The results of a 1963 survey taken to describe the state of social science information services in the United States (as reported by Jack Ferguson) provided one conceptual model. Ferguson used Machlup's economic model of inputs, processes, and outputs with the added dimension, "purpose," to discuss information organizations and their functions. Questionnaires were sent to 4,397 libraries, research organizations, public associations, and state and federal government agencies in order to gather descriptions of their information activities, types of materials collected or produced, details of services offered, publications, and types of users. Ferguson organized responses in a typology using Machlup's characteristics in order to avoid the complications of subject classification. Dimensions used were characterization of inputs as "literature" or "data"; characterization of processing as "collecting" or "transforming"; and characterization of the organization itself as "initiator" or "facilitator" of the work of others. The literature/data characterization (Figure 4-1) is shown as four cells: input may be literature and output may be literature, as in a library; or if the input is of one type and the output is another type, then some sort of transformation has taken place, which moves the subject to the second dimension (Figure 4-2).[14]

A generalized model of a rationalized social science information system, devised by Dan Bergen in 1967, exposed weakness in the then existing system. Bergen treated the problems of access to social science

Figure 4-1: Production Typology for Information Sources

COLLECT

Input	Output	
	Literature	Data
Literature	Library	
Data		Museum Data Bank Archives

TRANSFORM

Input	Output	
	Literature	Data
Literature	State of the art reviewing Abstracting & Translating Service	Content Analysis Center
Data	Research Organization	Statistics organization

Figure 4-2: Organizational Typology for Information Sources

INITIATE RESEARCH

Input	Processing	
	Collects	Transforms
Literature		Content Analysis Center
Data		Research organization

FACILITATE RESEARCH

Input	Processing	
	Collects	Transforms
Literature	Library	State of the art reviewing Abstracting & Translating Services
Data	Public Museum Data Bank Archives	Statistics Organization

Source: Jack Ferguson, *Specialized Social Science Information Services in the United States*, Clearinghouse for Federal Scientific and Technical Information, PB 167 841, p. VII 5.

knowledge in systemic terms, including both the bibliographic ("A") and personal ("B") exchange systems. In his model, managers of "A" (librarians and scholars) operate with incomplete information regarding "B." He observed that only thorough knowledge of the entire system would make way for a formalization of "B," and that such information was not currently available.[15]

Another modeling of the social science information system was provided by Ralph L. Bisco (Figure 4-3) in 1967. Specifically designed to demonstrate the role of the data archive in the social science information system, his model depicted various components of the system and indicated possible future developments in the relationships between the components.[16]

Because M. B. Line's 1969 discussion of information requirements in the social sciences served as a prelude to the most important social sciences user study yet conducted (INFROSS),[17] it deserves rather more detailed consideration than the efforts already mentioned.[18] Line included in his model of the social sciences information system those areas of knowledge concerned with human beings interacting or acting in groups. He noted that a kind of information system exists: libraries, cataloguers, bibliographers, indexing and abstracting journals, statistical collections, and data banks. Based on preliminary interviews with social scientists, he found that awareness of these sources was quite limited. Line first questions whether it is desirable to have a social sciences information system as a whole. He then notes that the overlap and commonality of the social science disciplines would make such a system desirable due to the wide scattering of social sciences citations in research reports among the various social sciences.[19]

Line sees this as implying that any really thorough service for social scientists would need to be based on a very large body of material. In addition, certain characteristics of the social sciences create a wide information need. These include the enormously varied nature of the social sciences, the interrelatedness of the social sciences, the newness and lack of definition of the social sciences, the instability of their terminology and the actual subjects of study, and the conceptual element of the social sciences.

Line's model of the social science information system is concerned with the relationship between three factors: users (or potential users); types of need; and possible solutions. He groups users into two basic categories: function and environment.

Function may be research, teaching and training, management, social work, the press, politics, business, or study and learning. *Environment* may be an academic institution, research organization, industry, government, professional association, trade union and political party, or the

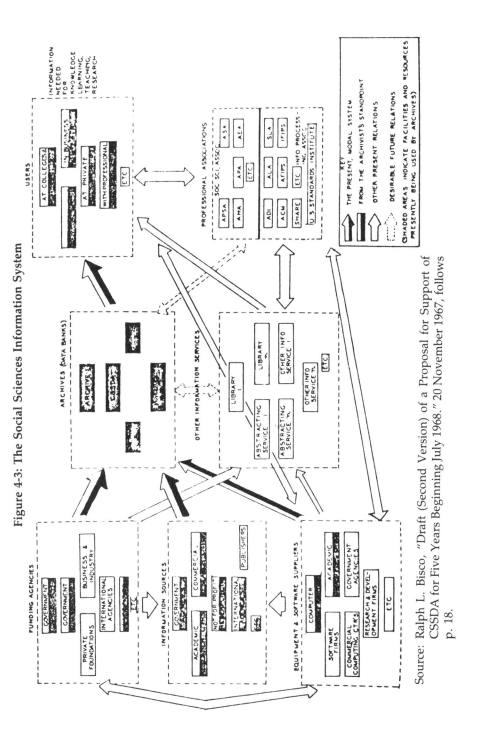

Figure 4-3: The Social Sciences Information System

Source: Ralph L. Bisco, "Draft (Second Version) of a Proposal for Support of CSSDA for Five Years Beginning July 1968." 20 November 1967, follows p. 18.

press. A subsidiary classification of users is by pure, applied, or practitioner-oriented research. Individual characteristics such as age, experience, work environment, awareness of sources of information and language skills also must be considered.[20]

Line distinguished between the study of the *individual user* (largely the psychology of information use) and the study of *users in groups* (the sociology of information use). In order to obtain a complete picture of the information system operating for a particular group, informal communication must be examined. The most complete examination of informal communication patterns in the social sciences thus far has focused on psychologists.[21]

Types of need may be considered from various aspects: a) subject content; b) nature of information—conceptual, theoretical, historical or statistical; c) quantity of need; d) processing—the various ways in which information can be presented; e) physical form of the information; f) speed of supply; g) data range; h) specificity; i) immediate function; j) quality; k) level.[22] Solutions to the problem, as identified by Line include:

- Bibliographies (specialized or general)
- Abstracting journals
- Indexing journals (traditional)
- "Current contents"
- Review publications
- "Newspapers" (e.g., New Society)
- Citation indexes
- Announcements of articles accepted for publication
- Lists and indexes of films, tapes, etc.
- Library collections
- Data banks
- Specialized documentation and information centers
- Abstracts or indexes issued in unit record form (e.g., commercially provided optical coincidence cards)
- SDI (whether national or local)
- Facsimile transmission
- Translation services
- Lists of research, etc., in progress
- Direct access to computer-stored information
- Personalized information service (e.g., local information officers)
- Informal channels[23]

Line's model (Figure 4-4) looked at the system as a whole in order to present the optimum relationship between methods of access to information. In addition to basic information, he considered access at four

**Figure 4-4: Access to Information: A General Model
of the Existing Formal System**

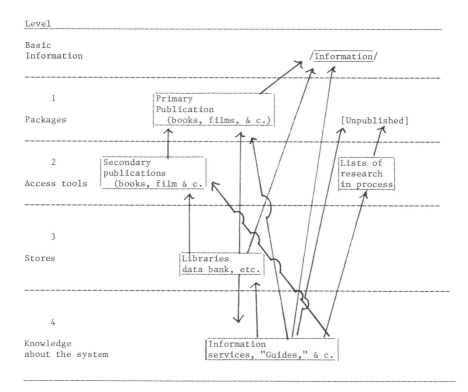

Source: Maurice B. Line, "Information Requirements in the Social Sciences:
Some Preliminary Considerations." *Journal of Librarianship* 1 (January
1969): 15.

levels: primary (packages); secondary (published access tools); tertiary
(stores, containing both primary and secondary materials); and a fourth
level—the means of obtaining knowledge about other levels.

More recent discussion indicates efforts toward greater inclusiveness
for social science information systems. White's 1973 observations on the
structure of the social information system noted that the system had
succeeded in filling some of the lacunae identified in the Chicago study,
namely, abstracting services to keep abreast of the literature and bibliographical reviews to keep abreast of progress in the field as a whole.[24] He
did not mention the problem of sources of data, however, except to
provide a compendium of sources of statistics. In that same year, Freides

clearly distinguished between literature (writings intended to analyze and comment on social life) and data (the written records of society). However, she did not discuss those data sources that originate outside of the social scientists' communication system.[25] Today we are no closer to having acceptable schemata of the social science information system, although the reasons for the system's diffuseness are better understood. J. M. Brittain noted in 1979 that this derives in part from the fact that the social sciences make do with information services modelled on the physical sciences and that great improvements could be made by gearing information services more closely to the specific communication patterns of the social sciences.[26] He suggested that further study is required to convince users that information flow and communication as well as the structure of knowledge in the social sciences are significantly different from those in the physical sciences. It is necessary to study (*inter alia*) the structure of knowledge, the relationship of formal communications, a systematic analysis of cited items, and the development of theories and schools of thought in the various social sciences.[27]

After explaining ways in which the social sciences vary from the physical sciences in terms of theoretical approach, Brittain observed:

It now seems unlikely that a totally non-scientific or a totally scientific approach, will ever exist. A mixture of both has always characterized social science and is likely to continue to do so. Information systems need to reflect this and it is useful if different types of social science can be described and appropriate information and documentation services made available, to match....

Structured information (in the form of knowledge) is most heavily in demand in social science research and education. At the other extreme, in applied work (e.g., in industry, government agencies, hospital, etc.) information needs are of a very different order. In the past we may have made the mistake of believing that an information system and library can serve all groups of users, but this is hardly possible.

There is now enough evidence from user studies to show that the majority of social scientists are not happy with the formal communication system which includes journals, monographs and secondary literature (Brittain, 1970). Social scientists are notoriously ignorant of existing information tools, they show a very strong dislike of using them, and they do not use them very effectively. Although many have been willing to go along with conventional information systems, based upon those successful in the sciences, the fact that social scientists are fairly ignorant of information services, and use them with reluctance, suggests that they intuitively find the substantial amount of effort required to have relatively little pay-off.[28]

This cogent and difficult assessment by Brittain indicates that it is probably untenable to try to develop a comprehensive model of the social science information system. To speak of a system implies a somewhat monolithic lock-step approach on the part of social scientists to their research, and clearly this is not the way in which social research is conducted.

In spite of the fact that those, such as Brittain, at the forefront of identification of the social science information system are beginning to doubt that such a system can be clearly diagrammed, it is helpful, for the purpose of this discussion, as it impinges on machine-readable social data, to continue as if diagramming is a possibility, if only to enable us to articulate the components—disregarding, for the time being, the efficiency of their interaction. The one component which receives little discussion in overall considerations of the system, the data archive or data library as a repository for machine-readable statistical data, is the component we wish to highlight here in order to identify ways in which it relates to the larger (if ill-defined) system.

Data Aspects of the Social Science Information System

The data aspects of the social science information system have come under greater scrutiny recently, due mainly to the intensive focus on specific problems of access to statistical numeric data by the International Association for Social Science Information Service and Technology (IASSIST). This organizing of data professionals, who maintain service centers for numeric data into a thriving international association, and the subsequent cross-fertilization of ideas between those involved in traditional/humanistic services and those involved in behavioral/quantitative services, has initiated renewed dialog and linkage between the two heretofore separate components of the system.[29]

Also, the focus on statistical data derives in part from a growing awareness of the variant types (as distinguished by Vondran, Smalley, Robbin, and others) of information seekers.[30] Essentially, these analysts of the social science information system have identified the research behavior of quantitative or behaviorally oriented social scientists as being quite different from traditional or humanistically oriented researchers. The dichotomy between types of users has been exacerbated by the rather specialized responses on the parts of the information system that have arisen to respond to the needs of the nontraditional users. The chasm that exists between the two types of responses has been bridged by only a few library and information specialists. The need to create a rapprochement has been voiced by Robbin, but conceptualization of the division must be understood before this can take place.[31]

In his study of academic historians, Vondran found that those who used the quantitative method behaved more like social scientists in their need for more recent literature than those using nonquantitative methods of research. The latter also made greater use of journals and relied on informal channels of communication.[32] Smalley's discussion of traditional and behavioral political scientists examined their different orientations and approaches to the research material. Her sketches of the variant research processes used by the two types of political scientists, while not characterized by her as a model of the political science sector of the social science information system, do, in some ways, characterize the dualistic nature of that system as a function of the approach of the researcher—a point also made by Vondran.[33]

The most comprehensive description of the complexity of the social science information system (especially for statistical data) is that provided by Robbin.[34] She concentrates on a typology of users which moves us closer to understanding the behaviorist social science information system described by Smalley. Robbin notes that the infrastructure for numerical data can be characterized as inchoate. Further,

Most producers of machine-readable data files have neither the resources nor expertise to preserve, maintain and distribute their data. They do not have established procedures for easy access to and inexpensive use of their data. Few data producers can supply adequate user support services related to teaching, research coordination of multiple research projects, computation and general information services related to machine-readable data files, which are often by-products of large data-gathering projects.

Primary and secondary information services either do not exist or provide limited information and data services in local environments. Few libraries have integrated the numerical data base into their collections, although it can logically be considered another information resource. As a result, the traditional abstracting and indexing services and other tools and services which serve a document-based community do not exist for numerical data. With few exceptions, data libraries have grown up outside the traditional library, without the foundation of generations of experience in providing technical and public service. Data libraries typically exist as adjuncts of social science departments and have not employed trained specialists in information management.[35]

Robbin provides a list of reasons for the lack of organization of the system as well as suggestions for its improvement. She observes that the social science information system is complicated by the multi-dimensionality of the problem-solving approach and requires an information support structure integrated along the same dimensions as the intellectual problem-solving activity.[36]

A Revised Model of the Social Science Information System

Recognizing the difficulties inherent in modeling the social science information system, especially given the qualifications cited above, this chapter nevertheless has attempted to provide a framework for a discussion of the role of governmental statistical machine-readable data for social scientists (Figure 4-5).

In this model, social science data are characterized as "Ur-documents" at the initial level. These are the raw materials for social scientific research. Included here are letters, diaries; verbatim proceedings of conferences, trials, or government hearings; video-tapes or films of actual events, data collected by polling agencies such as Roper or Harris, and, especially important for this discussion, statistical data gathered by governments and made available in either paper or machine-readable form. This material is then used by scholars, researchers and report writers at the "Intellectual Transformation" level to generate articles, books, government reports, or analyze polling information such as that broadcast by mass media. After the intellectual transformation takes place, the Ur-documents are then reorganized in a packaged form: books, articles, reports, edited films, or data tapes with technical documentation.

These packages are then subjected to a bibliographic transformation to make them retrievable through local standard storage sites. Librarians will catalog books and check-in serials, archivists will develop local catalogs, and data archivists/librarians will devise access to data tapes through their own catalogs. Once identifiable bibliographically, and thus retrievable at any given local storage site, a system transformation takes place for bibliographic control of the package at a nationally or internationally retrievable level.

At the system level there are some dysfunctions. Monographs can be identified through union catalogs or online systems such as OCLC or RLN; articles can be identified through indexing and abstracting services; technical reports can be identified through such services as NTIS or ERIC. Even archival materials have some degree of system control through union catalogs or subject directories. Machine-readable statistical data, however, have no mechanism for systemic identification. If the material has been printed on paper, it may be picked up by indexing services such as the *American Statistics Index* or the *Statistical Reference Index*, but the enormous amount of information in machine-readable format is only identifiable through catalogs such as those compiled by ICPSR* or informal channels. The underdevelopment of the social science information system *vis-à-vis* machine-readable data is the reason for this examination of that component of the social scientists' information need.

---

*ICPSR, Inter-university Consortium for Political and Social Research, located at Ann Arbor, Michigan.

Figure 4-5: Social Science Information System

Indexing and Abstracting Tools (paper & online)
Review Articles
Union Catalogs of Monographs and Archive Materials
Referral by Colleagues
Citation Indexes
Bibliographies
(lists of research in progress)

"UNION LIST" TOOLS

SYSTEM TRANSFORMATION BY NETWORKERS, INDEXERS,
ABSTRACTORS & INVISIBLE COLLEGE

Access Tools	Site
Catalog	Library
Catalog	Paper Archives
Catalog	Data Library

RETRIEVABLE STORAGE SITE

BIBLIOGRAPHIC TRANSFORMATION BY MONOGRAPHIC AND
SERIALS CATALOGERS, PAPER AND DATA ARCHIVISTS

Books, Journal Articles
Technical Reports
Films, Govt. Reports
Datatapes with Technical Documentation

PACKAGES

INTELLECTUAL TRANSFORMATION BY SCHOLARS,
RESEARCHERS, REPORT WRITERS

UR-DOCUMENTS
unanalyzed statistics
letters, diaries, verbatim proceedings

The pieces are in place for systematic input of these data through the new cataloging rules which accommodate machine-readable data files. In addition, there are professional groups, such as IASSIST, working on this major gap in the system. Nonetheless, there is no formalized structure by which these data can be identified and accessed.[37] Thus, at this stage the need to understand the organization of the informal channels that must be exploited to ensure access to these data is critical, especially for government-generated, machine-readable statistical data. This model does not differ radically from those presented earlier, except that it treats informal access to the system as being as important as formal access, and it fixes data and the data archive as formal components in the system. However, as has been already noted, knowledge of the data aspect of the system is shared by very few. Most researchers requiring these data bypass structures developed by librarians and data professionals in order to acquire the materials themselves. It is the responsibility of librarians to understand this system, especially if they intend to provide for the information needs of the social scientist. The foregoing section has demonstrated the reasonableness of the request that librarians provide access to this type of information for library patrons— especially those in the social sciences. While we speak generally of access to a variety of data resources, the discussion here focuses on governmental information in machine-readable form.

PART II: ACCESS TO STATISTICAL DATA

Failure of Traditional Libraries to Provide Access to Primary Data

Traditional library service to the researcher has largely concentrated on providing information packages in the form of books, periodicals, and microforms. While this service has suited the needs of those researchers requiring published material, those requiring data from the direct observation of phenomena have had to turn to other types of information facilities. Such accommodations have been made outside the traditional library for certain types of needs—all of which require access to some form of primary data. Thus, the humanist has had to rely on specialized manuscript collections; the historian, on archives; the scientist, on computer banks of numeric information; and the quantitative social scientist, on machine-readable data files stored in facilities such as data libraries.

Because the facilities that support the use of primary data have grown up outside of, or tangential to, the traditional library, they have not been the object of much study on the part of those who study information provision. Thus, little research is available detailing who the users of such facilities are; what type of packaging they prefer for their data;

what sort of support services they require to make optimal use of their data; or how their needs for these primary data can be met by established systems of information delivery.

Advanced technology has enhanced the capacity of libraries to respond to information needs other than those satisfied by traditionally published information. The advent of automated circulation systems, shared online cataloging, and bibliographic online services are some of the ways that the traditional library has moved toward embracing all types of information needs within one umbrella facility.

It has not been a simple matter, however, for a traditional library to integrate those information services which have of necessity developed their own set of responses to users and their own methods of organization. While archives are generally in close physical proximity to traditional libraries, they have evolved a set of responses to users that cannot be easily integrated into the library's routines. The computer facilities that house information banks of numeric data for use by physical scientists are a logical extension of information provision, yet the technological and economic barriers to placing these facilities within the library militate against their integration in the near future. For similar reasons, statistical information now stored in data libraries for use by social scientists or housed in government offices is also unlikely to become part of the library's overall information system, though provision of it, too, is but a logical extension of basic information provision.

Each of these different responses to the information needs of researchers requires examination, if a consolidated information system is ever to exist. Before a total information system accessible from one location can be developed, each part of the extant information system must be examined to discover the special needs of special users and to identify the points at which services are duplicated or converge with the services of the traditional library.

One of these fugitive information responses is the social science data archive or data library. This facility developed outside the traditional library because the traditional library was not ready to respond when the researchers' need arose. Put simply, the data library is the existing response by social science to its own need for stores of raw statistical data.

A data library contains a machine-readable collection of such information as survey, census, polling or legislative voting data. It is a laboratory for the social scientist, since it stores raw data for analysis of issues in social research and behavorial policy. Data collected by one agency or research team for one purpose may be preserved with appropriate documentation for the use of other researchers with an entirely different set of purposes. While archival preservation of such statistical data might seem to be an appropriate service for traditional libraries to offer, the need for such a facility emerged nearly a decade before libraries were able to respond with any type of mechanized information delivery.[38] Thus the data library has grown up as an information service usually funded by government agencies, academic social science departments, or consortia of universities. Outstanding archives include the Roper Center, the Inter-university Consortium for Political and Social Research, and the National Opinion Research Center as well as other installations at large universities such as the University of Wisconsin-Madison, Princeton, and the University of Illinois. But data libraries are relatively rare manifestations of an institutional response to the social scientist's need for statistical data. Fully developed data libraries providing the necessary services to support social science research exist at only a handful of universities and independent centers. In these times of tighter budgets, it seems unlikely that any but the best-funded academic institutions will continue to support this special service to social scientists.[39]

Although a small number of data libraries and consortia exists to which the librarian might refer patrons, very often librarians (even in an institution supporting a data library) may be unaware of them. Moreover, researchers requiring such materials are usually alerted to them through colleagues or other informal channels and bypass the library entirely.[40] The failure of librarians to make bibliographic linkages even when facilities exist on the same campus illustrates the librarians' poor response to this basic resource for social research, in spite of the fact that the data library is an important component in the social science information system as it has been modelled here.

There are really two levels, then, of librarians' potential response to the social scientists' need for raw data: referral to extant organizations and, in the absence of this option, mediation to obtain the data for the patron. It is because so many of these data are government-produced that this chapter focuses on this problem.

Federal Government Policy for Machine-Readable Statistical Data

Before describing methods for identifying and acquiring machine-readable governmental information, it is important to summarize Federal policy on this issue. It is not a simple matter to make such data usable. In addition to a policy of simple access, adjunct support services are required to make the information usable. The following discussion will update and expand on the papers, "Federal Statistical System: Access and Dissemination" and Joseph W. Duncan's "Accessing Social Statistics."[41]

Current Federal Policy

The current official statement by the Federal government appeared in the *Statistical Reporter* in March of 1981.[42] It is called "A Federal Policy for Improving Data Access and User Services," and updates the chapter on "User Access to Federal Public Data Files," which appeared in *A Framework for Planning U.S. Federal Statistics for the 1980's*.[43] The policy statement was developed under the aegis of the Office of Federal Statistical Policy and Standards (OFSPS), which was then part of the Department of Commerce and is now under the Office of Management and Budget. It was based on the deliberations of the Interagency Committee on Data Access and Use, a committee formed to develop and recommend policies and procedures to assure effective access to, and use of, federal statistical data and to provide a forum for federal agencies to exchange information and ideas concerning data access and use. The committee consists of representatives from departments with major statistical programs: Agriculture, Commerce, Education, Energy, Health and Human Services, Interior, Justice, Labor, and the Treasury.

The policy statement notes that the problems of ensuring access to federally collected statistical data and providing adequate services to those who use the data are among the most serious facing federal statistics in the 1980s.[44] These problems include: (1) data users' confusion and exasperation in trying to locate existing federal statistics; (2) agency personnel's opinion that for every actual data user they encounter many others need federal statistics but are unaware that they are available from the government; (3) sophisticated users' complaints of lengthy delays and time-consuming obstacles in obtaining federal data in usable form; and (4) some original data collection efforts launched to collect data already available (or which could have been readily available) from an existing data base.[45]

The policy statement is a response to a demand for greater access to statistics for use in all sectors of public and private life. The federal statistics system has responded piecemeal to this demand because of its decentralized nature, but nonetheless coordination is imperative:

Users need more centralized facilities for determining what data are available, their attributes, and how to obtain them. The welter of agencies producing statistics and making them available in a bewildering range of formats and according to widely varying rules and procedures constitutes a major frustration for the public.[46]

The statement continues that given these conditions, "it is incumbent upon the Federal statistical system to develop a coordinated, coherent and unified approach to the general problem of data access."[47] Data access, a nebulous term, is not defined but used to mean a variety of responses to the need for data in all its forms.

Although statistical agencies have always answered public inquiries, developed reference materials, and published statistical data, new social and technological changes are affecting data access. Traditional users still need responses, but a sophisticated elite demands data on a continuing day-to-day basis for use with their own computer. The need for data at a level of geographical detail not found in printed publications, as well as greater emphasis on planning requiring statistics, also increases the demand for access to federal statistical data.

This growing demand for access to machine-readable data files means that users can enjoy greater possibilities of data manipulation and access, applying different forms of statistical modeling and software not contemplated by the originating agency.

The release of statistical data in machine-readable format means that the user must have the technical expertise and financial and computer resources necessary to conduct retrievals and analysis. Those without such facilities do not, in effect, have equal access. The policy statement is a strong one, advocating the use of these files and calling for a change from the prevailing agency attitude. From "Here are our statistics; if you wish to use them, come to us and we will assist you if it is not too much trouble for us," to a more activist stance—"Here are your statistics, please let us help you to use them." The statement observes that the prevailing perspective ignores the fact that not all users are able to articulate effectively, or have little conception of all their needs, and are unaware of the data holdings of federal agencies. Although the federal statistical system is fairly well-equipped to serve those who know and can articulate their needs, many potential users who cannot cross this threshold of knowledge and communication are ill-served.[48] It is at this point that the informed documents librarian can intercede most effectually for all patrons and specifically for the social scientist.

The OFSPS sets forth in great detail its responsibility for lowering the threshold of knowledge needed to approach the system, maximization of awareness, and for the use and application of the statistics in which the public has invested. Nonetheless, it seems appropriate that, just as documents professionals have sought to intercede on behalf of their constituency for better use of paper and microfiche documents, so they should seek to intercede for better use of machine-readable files.

The beginning of this process is full appreciation of the federal government's efforts to enhance the use of these materials. Once documents librarians understand the efforts of the federal government, they can make decisions about where to intervene in the system on behalf of users and potential users. As the policy statement points out, systematic attention to the questions of data access and user services on the part of federal agencies is an integral part of the Paperwork Reduction Act of 1980.

1980 OFSPS Survey of Data Access Practices

The bulk of the official policy statement under discussion is based on an informal survey of the data access practices of the agencies represented by the Interagency Committee on Data Access and Use. For each item examined, the OFSPS statement provides discussion and "recommended good practice," in the form of general standards against which agencies can measure their performance.

Policy Developments. Executive Order 12013 established a Statistical Policy Coordination Committee (SPCC) to provide Cabinet-level advice on matters of statistical policy requiring consideration by the President.[49] It was this Committee which elevated the topic of improved access to federal statistical data to the status of a cross-cutting issue in the FY 1982 budget and gave high priority to developing data access policy and improved mechanisms for meeting user needs.[50] The OFSPS established the Interagency Committee on Data Access and Use in response to the SPCC recommendations.[51]

— *Recommended Good Practice:* In recognition of the diversity of the Federal statistical system (some agencies deal exclusively with statistical data, while others have statistical units) and the variegated organizational circumstances of federal statistics, the following general policies for the statistical agencies and agencies with statistical units were recommended:
1. Engagement in promotional activities to provide users with improved access to federally collected data and with such services as will enable them to utilize better the data.
2. Examination of basic policies underlying their data access and user service programs to ensure that these policies include an active marketing outreach toward the user.
3. Development of procedures for routinely examining the costs and benefits of releasing their data holdings to the public.
4. Development of procedures for routine interaction with user communities, for making users aware of agency data holdings, and for measuring user demand for data.
5. Protection of privacy and confidentiality, and provision of the resources to maintain adequate user services for the files of those agen-

cies which have already taken the steps to inform users and have ascertained that there is a demand.[52]

Organization and Budgeting for the Data Access Function. The OFSPS survey found only two agencies with an identifiable budget for data access: the Bureau of the Census, which has a Data User Services Division, and the Bureau of Justice Statistics (under contract with the University of Michigan). In spite of the SPCC's insistence on the importance of data access, this function has not gained sufficient bureaucratic identity within the federal statistical system. A first step to move toward this goal is deployment of agency personnel to create specific, identifiable organizational units charged with the data access function along with budgetary resources.

— *Recommended Good Practice*:
1. Designation of a specific organizational unit and specific personnel whose major responsibility is the improvement of data access and user services within each agency or unit for statistical agencies.
2. Designation of personnel for the improvement of data access and use for nonstatistical units.[53]

Informational and Reference Services. Only half of the agencies surveyed provided brochures describing data holdings and four had newsletters for data users. The discussion includes the observation:

A major service of the Federal statistical system would be a more systematic, coherent program for dissemination of information about data sources, contacts and responsibilities. At present, numerous areas attempt to provide such support with little coordination. These include one-time announcements in various publications generally designed to service other needs as well, flyers and agency brochures. Such approaches are often not conducive to maintaining and disseminating such information in an organized manner.[54]

Specific issues for newsletter development include coverage by field of researchers, greater frequency of publication, and an orientation to the needs of users.

Although most agencies publish catalogs or lists of publications, they should move to develop catalogs with classified lists of bibliographic abstracts; published indexes and table findings guides with references to individual table levels rather than to single data bases; and computerized indexing and query systems. The development of subject-matter directories to assist users in locating statistical information irrespective of originating agency, in a mode similar to *American Statistics Index*, is on the horizon. The National Center for Health Statistics' *Facts at Your Fingertips* and the National Center for Education Statistics' *Directory of Federal Agency Education Tapes* are examples of government-produced sources that simplify the information search for users unfamiliar with the complex organization of the federal statistical system.[55] Reference materials should adopt a stronger user orientation through such efforts as developing simplified standard error tables and examples of application to the more conventional theoretical discussions of sampling variation as well as concept definitions written to anticipate user questions and problems. These materials should be well written with good documentation of codebooks. Unreleased data should be described, and all information should be updated regularly.[56]

— Recommended Good Practice:
1. Publication of flyers and brochures describing statistics and means of access.
2. Publication of reference materials containing technical guidance for the use of the data on a regular basis.
3. Establishment of newsletters for sophisticated users.
4. Development of adequate documentation for data files available on a restricted basis.
5. Systematization of dissemination of information about available data.
6. Development of access tools on major topics, irrespective of agency.[57]

Inquiry Services. One of the main problems encountered by data users is that there is no coordinated starting point for statistical inquiries. Agencies vary in the quality and focus of the services they provide. Two agencies, the Bureau of the Census and the Bureau of Labor Statistics, have developed regional inquiry services in major cities. Both the National Center for Education Statistics and National Center for Health Statistics operate centralized inquiry services, which function as switching centers for all national inquiries. Four agencies, the Bureau of the Census, Bureau of Labor Statistics, the Economic and Statistics Service of the Department of Agriculture, and the Energy Information Administration, publish brochures with a subject-matter breakdown of statistics keyed to individuals within the agency. However, while the major statistical agencies have such systems, agencies which are nonstatistical in overall mission do not have such services and evoke considerable frustration in users.

The OFSPS has published the *Federal Statistical Directory* listing names, offices, and telephone numbers of key personnel in statistical activities in all Departments (the most recent edition, published in 1979, was a Department of Commerce publication: SuDoc # C 1.75). OFSPS had planned to restructure the next edition of the *Directory* in three levels. Level 1, a single contact for information and publications for each agency, was published in the October 1980 issue of the *Statistical Reporter*; Level 2 would have been a subject matter listing for major statistical programs; and Level 3, the *Directory* as a previously issued format with the possibility of computerization for ease of updating. However, recent changes and budget cuts in the OFSPS, which include the demise of the *Statistical Reporter* in January 1982, make the future of the *Directory* uncertain.

— *Recommended Good Practice*:
1. Federal statistical agencies should have a public inquiry service to answer queries from the general public as well as to offer brochures indicating telephone contacts.
2. Statistical agencies in nonstatistical departments without query services should make use of the larger inquiry system to ensure that statistical queries are well handled.
3. Routine logging of inquiries for management purposes should be considered.
4. Sensitization of staff to proper attitudes in the handling of public inquiries.[58]

Promotional and Marketing Services. Press releases provide a common mechanism for dissemination of information about new data, but since access information is not "newsworthy," this usually fails to filter down to the user. *Articles in professional journals*, as well as trade publications or papers given at professional meetings, often prepared for specific interest groups, are another strategy for generating information about new data, but depend on the skills and orientation of individual agency personnel rather than an overall agency information program. *Exhibit booths* at conferences of professional societies are used extensively by the Census Bureau, but not as routinely by other agencies due to cost and lack of visible payoff. *Direct-mail promotion* is undertaken by many agencies and, on occasion, *purchase of mailing lists* of professional associations. *Advertising* in publications has chiefly been restricted to the cross-advertising of one statistical publication in another and has not reached a substantially new audience. Paid advertising is rare. A number of guidelines regarding agency publication programs are treated. These include the need for *comprehensive coverage* and promotion of the full range of data products with general utility, the need for use of a *variety of media* and *creative designing* of advertisements. *Data applications* are also viewed as important in the development of publicity since to generate significant interest users should have an idea of possible applications, practical uses of the data, and reasons for their initial collection.[59]

Examples of agency publicity materials that emphasize data applications are the Bureau of the Census brochure, *Census Data for Community Action* and the Social Security Administration's "Policy Analysis with Social Security Research File." However, these are rare examples of what should be a general promotional effort on the part of agencies.[60]

User training programs which provide information on data access and use include the National Center for Health Statistics' series of workshops for medical and health science librarians at state and regional meetings; the Energy Information Administration's one-day and tutorial seminars; the Bureau of Labor Statistics' training courses for its data management system, LABSTAT; and the Social Security Administration's Office of Research and Statistics' conferences on the Continuous Work Sample.[61]

The broadest based program for the promotion of resources through user training programs is that of the Bureau of the Census. It offers a variety of conferences, seminars, workshops and courses targeted toward federal, state, and local government personnel and librarians. The Census Bureau's State Data Center Program, a cooperative data-dissemination and user service program involving the Bureau and participating states, has also provided substantial training as well as inquiry services, orientation and consultation, tape processing and analytical support for data use. Since October 1980, the *Statistical Reporter* has carried information on the training activities of federal statistical agencies, but with the demise of that important periodical the future of such announcements is unclear.

Other training issues discussed include the need for training techniques that take advantage of the principles of good teaching; for special attention to be given to audiences (such as college teachers or librarians) in a position to convey the knowledge gained to potential users; and for the preparation for self-study materials for those users unable to attend conferences.

— *Recommended Good Practice*:
1. Management of mailing lists to reduce costs and reach target populations effectively.
2. Use of paid advertising where appropriate.
3. Development of materials describing the applications.
4. Consideration of user training as an integral part of a full data access program.[62]

Machine-Readable Data Files. Although machine-readable data files are important and valuable for researchers, policy-makers and administrators, they are vastly under-utilized. Identifying, assessing, acquiring, and using these files is hindered at every step by a dearth of information about them. Regardless of the user's field of research, a way is needed to impart what files exist, what data they contain, and how best to use them. These files are "invisible" to potential users and are usually segregated from other sources of information. In many federal agencies, data-file dissemination activities are far removed from traditional "hardcopy" data-distribution mechanisms.[63] These difficulties are accentuated by the fact that thirty-eight different federal agencies are involved in data-producing activities, each with independent authority over its own data programs, procedures, and statistical objectives. Inconsistency in policy partially derives from the different legal mandates of each agency for production and distribution of files and different perceptions as to responsibilities in assisting users.

The OFSPS survey found that, except for the Bureau of Mines and the Energy Information Administration, all agencies queried released machine-readable data files to the public. The number of files issued varied from 15 to 1,200 per agency and the number of copies of each from several hundred to 3,000. Documentation, of varying quality, was also available from each agency.

Half of the agencies handled their own file dissemination, while others used NTIS, NARS, or a combination. Only two agencies issued software. The National Center for Health Statistics is considering providing sample data sets at the front of large files, and the National Center for Educational Statistics provides users with control cards for SPSS and SAS as well as machine-readable codebooks at the front of some of its files. Special initiatives include data-tape users conferences by the National Center for Health Statistics; the Census Bureau's State Data Center Program; and the Social Security Administration's workshop on Social Security Files for Policy Analysis.[64]

Documentation of files continues to be a problem. Only half of the agencies surveyed had agency documentation standards, and *no standardization exists across agencies*. The single federal statistical publication which offers guidelines for technical documentation of statistical machine-readable files is Richard C. Roistacher's *A Style Manual for Machine-Readable Data Files and Their Documentation*, published by the Bureau of Justice Statistics.[65] Without good technical documentation of bibliographic control standards, no coordinated system of information services can be created for machine-readable data files. The process of developing data access and user services must include the development and enforcement of standards governing bibliographic abstracts and documentation. Key issues for documentation are *completeness, availability, packaging, updating*, and the *quality and consistency of abstracting and indexing*.

The OFSPS has introduced a new statistical policy directive requiring agencies to follow a uniform standard for bibliographic entries and abstracts. The *Directory of Federal Statistical Data Files*, issued in March, 1981 and available from NTIS, will, perhaps, generate some consistency in this area.[66]

File release procedures have not been established by all agencies. Almost no agency surveyed by OFSPS had an agencywide procedure for deciding if and when particular files should be released.

— *Recommended Good Practice*:
1. Special attention must be devoted to the problem of adequate abstracting and technical documentation for public use machine-readable data files. Each agency should establish and enforce standards for technical documentation.
2. Establishment of procedures for determining whether and when public use machine-readable data files should be released.
3. Application of standards for timeliness of release should follow the same standards for machine-readable data files as for printed publication.[67]

Issues for the Future

The OFSPS policy statement also addressed a number of more complicated issues *vis-à-vis* the problems of access to machine-readable statistical data. These are second-level considerations, and become of greater importance once responsibility for primary use and initial access has been accomplished.

Provision of Software and Other Aids. Access to the data and support in its use is an important first step in the federal government's promotion of its machine-readable data. However, because of the complexities of making use of data from the files, retrieval systems for the information are also desirable. Some agencies do this already, such as the Energy Information Administration's software package to accompany its Applied Analysis Models; and the Bureau of the Census' provision of CENSPAC for retrieval from machine-readable census files. Problems may arise in the provision of software insofar as this might infringe upon the private sector. The Bureau of Labor Statistics found that its LABSTAT system was called into question by private vendors, who argued that while federal agencies are a unique resource for the provision of federally collected data, they should not develop aids that infringe upon the products of the private sector.[68]

Pricing. No uniform standards exist for the pricing of government-produced machine-readable data files. Currently it is assumed that tape reproduction must be cost-effective but that original collection and processing are government responsibilities. This is a complex issue, and as demands for a full array of services for the various statistical agencies grow, this may be an area in which federal policy will shift.[69]

Off-loading Data Access Functions. As demand increases for machine-readable data files, and as adjunct services as well as internal resources for the development of those services dwindle, data access functions may be shifted to other agencies. The National Center for Health Statistics disseminates most of its data files through NTIS and the Bureau of Labor Statistics is considering a similar arrangement. The Bureau of Justice Statistics handles the dissemination of its public use files through the Inter-university Consortium for Political and Social Research at the University of Michigan, which maintains the Criminal Justice Archive and Information Network.[70]

User Surveys. More information is required about user needs. In 1978 the USDA Economics and Statistics Service contracted with the National Opinion Research Center to conduct a study in North and South Dakota of farm operators' opinions toward statistical and economic information. They have conducted similar surveys in subsequent years. The idea of surveying users to determine if information is effective is just coming into currency among federal agencies. More interaction is needed with users to determine their various requirements for satisfactory use of data. In general the OFSPS policy statement is one of strong advocacy for users of federally produced machine-readable statistical data.[71] If fully implemented, the recommendations for good practice would amount to an analog of the federal governmental structure for good dissemination of hardcopy materials. Not only would the files be available but they would be adequately documented, released on a regular basis, and accompanied by support services requisite to their total exploitation. However, recent Federal policy in the form of termination of key access tools to the system in general, such as the *Statistical Reporter*, cut at the heart of this extremely liberal statement for access. If the government lags in its support for access to these data, what alternative strategies exist for making them available to users?

Intervention of Documents Librarians in the Identification, Acquisition, and Exploitation of Federal Machine-Readable Statistical Data

The previous section has just examined current federal policy for the dissemination of statistical machine-readable data files. In spite of the tone of advocacy, the vision of a united front for the provision of multi-leveled access and the conceptual recognition of the needs of users noted in this policy, it is critical that documents librarians recognize the limitations of the extant system as it currently functions in order to be able to intervene in the system, speed it up, and make it work for users.

The first portion of this chapter emphasized the importance of statistical data in its raw form to social science research and the fact that provision of such data is as important to researchers as is provision of printed materials. Further, traditionally organized libraries have been unable to accommodate such material due to lack of an understanding of its nature and lack of the technical expertise to activate its use. Current strategies to obtain such data on the part of its users generally circumvent the traditional library in favor of data libraries or other repositories which facilitate the use of such material.

However, few institutions have fully developed data libraries and, even in those that do, it is the responsibility of the librarian to function, at the very least, as a bibliographic broker in the dissemination of information support for the exploitation of these files.[72] The remainder of this section will address what reasonable steps the documents librarian might take to create linkages between the federal statistical data sets available in machine-readable form and social science researchers requiring these data for their work.

Identification of Federal Statistical Machine-Readable Data

Documentation as a Means of Identification. As was observed in the discussion of the OFSPS policy statement, technical documentation of machine-readable data sets is still in its nascent stages. If the codebook and adjunct documentation of data sets were within the purview of the traditional publishing structures, these could be acquired, cataloged, and shelved in documents collections or by subject. These materials would then lead the user naturally to the next step—acquisition of the machine-readable files. However, the current state of documentation of these materials is inchoate.

The lack of standardization for documentation of machine-readable data files is a multi-faceted problem. As Alice Robbin points out:

It is critical that standards for data quality be established. Such standards must reflect the principle that statistical data represent objective and verifiable evidence that is unambiguously described, so that analysis or evaluation based on this evidence can be effectively reviewed, criticized and replicated.... Analysts need high-quality data and a documented history of the decisions regarding the design, collection, encoding, processing and reduction of data. Computer programmers need information on the data and decisions about computer processing that affected the file. Librarians are concerned about the bibliographical procedures that identify, describe, and locate the files. [Data] archivists need sufficient information to identify, arrange, and describe records. Sponsors need guidelines to inform their judgments about ways to organize, fund, and maintain the quality of data files and their documentation.[73]

If written documentation accompanied machine-readable files and provided a history of their development and contents, much of the obfuscation clouding them could be circumvented. The files would also be easier for librarians to integrate into extant library infrastructures. This documentation would describe the purpose of the file as well as the conceptual framework of the file's creators. It would be an integrated set of information, identifying, describing, clarifying, and providing access. Robbin's "Guidelines for Preparing and Documenting Data" are the first comprehensive standards to address the needs of analysts, computer programmers, librarians, archivists, and sponsors of data collections.[74] These are a convenient starting point for understanding the nature of machine-readable statistical files. This author advocates their perusal by documents librarians interested in functioning as intermediaries in the provision of these sources to social science users.

Part Three of Robbin's "Guidelines" describes bibliographical practices to ensure access to information about data files once they are available for release. Robbin notes:

Experience suggests that one of the greatest problems facing the secondary analyst is locating a file. We have found that standard bibliographical practices carried out by authors, publishers, libraries, and archives for printed materials have not been used by data producers.[75]

Thus, in spite of the fact that file-documentation mechanisms are beginning to be developed, it is still incumbent upon librarians seeking to act as information brokers to maintain a high level of general awareness of the variety of data in this format. Although we know what we can ideally expect (Robbin's "Guidelines"), we cannot expect to find this level of documentation at the present. In the interim, techniques for current awareness must be practiced.

Current Awareness of New Machine-Readable Files. As was pointed out in the OFSPS policy statement, machine-readable statistical files tend to be invisible due to lack of bibliographic control and documentation. However, a number of recent developments (in addition to Robbins' "Guidelines") have begun to solve this problem. For instance, the 1978 edition of the *Anglo-American Cataloging Rules* contains standards for the cataloguing of machine-readable data files, and created a mechanism for the inclusion of file-level access in library catalogs.[76] The arduous struggle to legitimize these files as bibliographic entities has been described by Sue A. Dodd in an article in the Winter 1982 issue of *Library Trends*.[77] However, no national cataloguing system can yet accommodate this information. Although the mechanism for bibliographic control at the file level is now in place, it is also important for those who serve users of such data to monitor a number of somewhat elusive publications for current awareness of files as they are released and updated. The publication in 1981 of the *Directory of Federal Statistical Data Files*[78] is, of course, an initial starting point for familiarity with the diversity and scope of government files. The numerous agency brochures, newsletters, and catalogs delineated in the *Statistical Reporter* supplement should also be scanned on a regular basis according to user demands and requirements.[79]

Commercial tools such as *ASI* will provide information about paper statistical publications which can be cross-verified with the *Directory* for machine-readable analogs. Even very general sources such as Kruzas' *Encyclopedia of Information Systems and Services*[80] or Wasserman's *Statistics Sources* [81] provide alerts to useful data bases.

NTIS' *Directory of Computerized Data File and Related Technical Reports* (SuDoc # C51.11/2:980-2); NARS' *Catalog of Machine-Readable Records in the National Archives of the United States* (SuDoc # G54.17/3:R24); and GAO's *Federal Information Sources and Systems: A Directory for the Congress* (SuDoc. # GA/.22:In3/980) also provide information about statistical files as general alerts. For a fee, DUALabs, an independent firm with NTIS ties, has set up an Information Documentation Center and will conduct a search of the federal statistics system.[82]

Outside of these sources, the newsletters, proceedings and miscellaneous publications of professional groups interested in the use of machine-readable data will also help documents librarians to become aware of data sets in demand. The two main groups to monitor are the International Association for Social Science Information Service and Technology[83] and the Association of Public Data Users.[84] It is still true that no one source (there is no analog of the *Monthly Catalog*) provides centralized monitoring of information for machine-readable data. Documents librarians desiring to serve the social science researcher as bibliographic brokers, however, will find that scanning the above mentioned publications will provide a broad understanding of the variety of machine-readable files available.

Acquisition and Exploitation of Federal Machine-Readable Statistical Data

Acquisition of these data is inextricably bound up with their exploitation. If a data library exists on a given campus, the procedure will be very different than if it does not. This section will first outline the steps the documents librarian might follow if such a facility exists. Discussion will then focus on what might be done if no facility is available locally.

Interaction with a Local Data Library. Prior to a decision to activate the intermediary function for federal machine-readable statistical information, the documents librarian should contact social science departments to identify those researchers invoofficial data library may exist on a given campus, it is likely that some sort of interim measure such as an informal tape library in the Department Chair's office exists. In the event that a full-fledged data library is present, it is important to make contact with the data professional in order to be apprised of his or her routines and policies.

These policies may pertain to the acquisition of machine-readable data. Generally the price of acquiring and maintaining these files is high, not only only in initial cost but in personnel needed to clean and reformat the data for compatability with local systems. The complexity of the data acquisition process has been addressed at length by Robbin in a paper entitled, "The Pre-Acquisition Process," in which she identified various factors for archives to consider before acquiring a given file.[85] These include type of project (coursework or research); length of time client has to complete the project; and status of the client.

Once the documents librarian has established the acquisition policy of the local data library s/he can decide at what level to field bibliographic inquiries for such data. In the long run it would be ideal if the human-readable documentation for each file acquired was located not only at the data facility but in the documents library as well. A good working relationship between the documents librarian brokering information about machine-readable statistical data and the data librarian deploying it is critical to an activist stance. Without such a relationship the two will be at cross-purposes and the client will be ill-served. If a data library exists, however, the documents librarian's responsibilities will probably end at the point of identification of the data's existence. The linkages between the two systems will be made, and the user can move on to his or her research.

Data Acquisition and Exploitation in the Absence of a Data Facility. If no formal or quasi-formal archive facility exists for the deployment of machine-readable statistical data, the documents librarian who has decided to provide information about this resource faces a number of problems. An internal policy decision must be made. Will the documents library establish the necessary linkages with other campus facilities to make the data usable? This generally requires a triumvirate of resources: (1) a locus for the acquisition and maintenance of the data; (2) the means to mount and make the data usable; (3) statistical consulting services to aid in the exploitation of the data. There are few campuses today where these three types of service do not exist. However, they usually function in isolation from one another for the purpose of facilitating the use of secondary data.

Should the library decide to take over the acquisition and maintenance of the data, not only will budget reorganization need to take place, but technical skills must be added to the documents librarian's professional repertoire or another individual with these skills must be added to the staff. Howard White, in his dissertation, "Social Science Data Sets: A Study for Librarians," has pointed out the complexities of this decision which militates against library assumption of such responsibilities in most cases.[86]

Even if this commitment were made, it would be necessary to work closely with the campus computing center and whatever statistical support is available to ensure full exploitation of the machine-readable data. The variety of users who seek such data will also cause difficulty. Just as users of printed material range from the freshman student requiring a few facts for a rhetoric paper to a highly knowledgeable professor requiring State Department dispatches for a scholarly thesis, so the level of skill of the users of machine-readable data will vary. If documents librarians intend to promote and make machine-readable data usable without the benefit of a full-service data facility, they must be ready to determine the type of individual they can and will serve. Thus, while it may be feasible to obtain statistical tapes for the professor already conversant with the problems of mounting and running a tape and subjecting it to sophisticated statistical tests, it may not be feasible to supply the same sort of support to the undergraduate attempting his or her first foray into secondary analysis.

The level of service, if such service is decided as appropriate to a documents department, may be thought of as a continuum. At the level of conservative service we would find the identification of data, and at the level of liberal service we might find the library mounting the same service as a fully developed data archive. Figure 4-6 demonstrates the continuum of services which might be offered by a documents department functioning in lieu of a data facility. Few libraries have developed full-service archives. An exception is the University of Florida, which operates a Data Library within a traditional library structure. This service, initiated in 1971 in response to needs for data from the 1970 Census of Population and Housing, organizes and services machine-readable data files purchased with library funds by any individual, department or group within the University. Ray Jones, describing this service, comments that users identify the university library as a source of information in all formats.[87]

Figure 4-6: Continuum of Data Services Which Might Be Provided by Documents Departments

Conservative	*Low Moderate*	*High Moderate*	*Liberal*
Identification of machine-readable data.	Assistance in obtaining data set with client's funds from grants or out-of-pocket.	Library purchase of data set and maintenance of files.	Library support of data use through acquisition; software and statistical support.

And that is really the central point of this discussion. Heretofore, librarians have tended to concentrate on printed materials with some attention to recorded and visual items. They continue to lag in satisfying the data needs of social science clientele. Documents librarians have the opportunity to recapture this function through facilitation of primary source material in the form of machine-readable data for the social scientist. Whether this function is done full-scale, as at the University of Florida, or in some more modest way through bibliographic brokering, is a difficult choice. However, to continue to shrug off (at the very least) bibliographic responsibility for the vast statistical resources of the federal government is to fail to provide access to a growing portion of government-produced information.

Conclusion

This chapter has examined the social sciences and their information system in order to place statistical information resources available in machine-readable form *squarely* as part of that system. It then summarized current federal policy regarding access to machine-readable government-produced data and suggested mechanisms and strategies by which librarians might augment access to this information resource. In light of all this, it may be difficult to keep a larger world-view in perspective as we exhort the already beleaguered documents librarian to add more duties and more responsibility to a position that is under seige due to the rising costs of materials, changing document formats, and increased government censorship of important items.

Perhaps, by mentioning the importance of the social science research which librarians support through information delivery, the task will not seem so onerous. In a paper entitled, "Information Management and Public Choice," Michael O'Hare observed:

Public policy decisions can err if the wrong set of preferences—and prices that describe them—are used to construct the objective function (the wrong problem is solved), or if the decision is made on the basis of bad information about the policy's consequences (the problem is solved wrong).[88]

O'Hare contends that information should be packaged for the user and the librarian made aware that different users will use it in different ways.[89] While he does not mention librarians in his discussion, one should recognize that astute librarians, able to process data produced by the government, will enable researchers to develop models specific to the problems they are examining.

Literature examining the impact of the social sciences upon public policy (such as the publications of the Association for Public Policy Analysis and Management, the long-term studies of the OECD on the relationships between the social sciences and decision-making bodies, and the National Research Council's Study Project on Social Research and Development) all contain discussions on the role of the social sciences in governmental decision-making.[90] As librarians come to recognize the growing impact of good social science research on governmental policy, the provision of machine-readable data, a key resource for the social sciences, becomes an increasingly important service to develop. While librarians may have to accommodate the services they can provide to local situations, and perhaps opt for a moderate rather than an activist stance in securing and aiding in the exploitation of these data, it is imperative that they choose to take some action.

Perhaps the easiest way to sum up the importance of library provision of these data is to take note of James H. Laue's remarks that the discipline of "sociology grew out of a concern for reform and social justice, a belief in the possibility (and for some the inevitability) of progress, and the often unexamined conviction that rationality and truth-telling can (and usually do) affect social policy in a positive direction."[91] According to Lane, sociologists' concept of the "just society" is a macro-social system in which:

- resources are allocated on the basis of equality rather than equity;

- interest groups (especially non-elitist groups) are sufficiently empowered to negotiate their own rights (i.e., power is diffused rather than centralized);

- decision making is orderly, patterned, democratic, and based on rationality and good data;

- the population is pluralistic in base and tolerant of pluralism in outlook (the world-view is cosmopolitan rather than local);

- the ultimate aim (and, ideally, the outcome) of the society's existence is maximum personal fulfillment for all persons in the system.[92]

Libraries can contribute to the third element necessary for a just society. Provision of data through the facilitation of access to machine-readable information to help achieve orderly, patterned, and democratic decision-making is another step toward this goal.

References

1. Robert F. Boruch, David S. Cordray and Paul M. Wortman, "Secondary Analysis: Why, How, and When," in *Reanalyzing Program Evaluations: Policies and Practices for Secondary Analysis of Social and Educational Programs*, Robert F. Boruch, Paul M. Wortman, and David S. Cordray, eds., (San Franciso: Jossey-Bass, 1981), p. 2.

2. Ibid., pp. 3-5.

3. J. M. Brittain and S. A. Roberts, "Information Services in the Social Sciences: Development and Rationalization," *International Social Science Journal*, 28(1976): 835.

4. Ibid.

5. Carl M. White, et al., *Sources of Information in the Social Sciences: A Guide to the Literature*, 2nd ed. (Chicago: American Library Association, 1973), p. 2.

6. Bert F. Hoselitz, ed., *A Reader's Guide to the Social Sciences*, rev. ed. (New York: The Free Press, 1970).

7. Thelma Freides, *Literature and Bibliography of the Social Sciences* (Los Angeles: Melville Publishing, 1973), p. 19.

8. Ibid.

9. D. J. Foskett, *Classification and Indexing in the Social Sciences* (London: Butterworths, 1974), pp. 19-20.

10. John Madge, *The Tools of Social Sciences* (London: Longmans, Green, 1953), as discussed in J. M. Brittain, *Information and Its Users* (Claverton Down, Bath: Bath University Press, 1970), pp. 36-37.

11. National Research Council Committee on Information in the Behavioral Sciences, *Communication System and Resources in the Behavioral Sciences* (Washington, D.C.: National Science Academy, 1967), p. 21.

12. Ibid., p. 22.

13. "Bibliographical Services in the Social Sciences," *Library Quarterly*, 20 (April 1950): 79-100.

14. Jack Ferguson, *Specialized Social Science Information Services in the United States* (Clearinghouse for Federal Scientific and Technical Information: PB 167 841).

15. Dan Bergen, "The Communication System of the Social Sciences," *College and Research Libraries*, 28 (July 1967): 239-252.

16. Ralph L. Bisco, "Draft (Second Version) of a Proposal for Support of CSSDA for Five Years Beginning July, 1968," November 20, 1967 (Mimeographed), follows p. 18.

17. The extensive research program into information problems and systems in the social sciences conducted at the University of Bath, between 1967 and 1975 included as its first major project an Investigation into Information Requirements of the Social Sciences (INFROSS). The full report was published by Bath University in 1971 in two volumes. A summary by M. B. Line appeared in *Aslib Proceedings*, 23 (August 1971): 412-434.

18. Maurice B. Line, "Information Requirements in the Social Sciences: Some Preliminary Considerations," *Journal of Librarianship*, 1 (January 1969): pp. 1-19.

19. Line partly bases his assertion on the Earle and Vickery 1965 *Aslib* study, which analyzed social science citations to obtain a quantitative indication of the use of social sciences literature. This is summarized in their article, "Social Science Literature Use in the UK as Indicated by Citations," *Journal of Documentation*, 25 (June 1969): 123-141.

20. Ibid., pp. 7-10.

21. Ibid., pp. 11-12.

22. American Psychological Association, *Reports of the American Pyschological Association's Project on Scientific Information Exchange in Psychology* (Washington, D.C.: American Psychological Association, 1965).

23. Line, "Information Requirements in the Social Sciences," pp. 13-14.

24. White, *Sources of Information in the Social Sciences*, p. 7.

25. Freides, *Literature and Bibliography of the Social Sciences*, p. 2.

26. J. M. Brittain, "Information Services and the Structure of Knowledge in the Social Sciences," *International Social Science Journal*, 31 (1979): 712.

27. Ibid., pp. 716-717.

28. Ibid., p. 723.

29. IASSIST publishes the *IASSIST Newsletter* (ISSN 0145-238X) and conference proceedings which discuss these issues in depth. See especially papers from the 1981 conference held in Grenoble, France, 14-18 September 1981, published by the Association under the title, *The Impact of Computerisation on Social Science Research*.

30. Raymond Florian Vondran, Jr., "The Effect of Method of Research on the Information Seeking Behavior of Academic Historians," Ph.D. dissertation, University of Wisconsin-Madison, 1976; Topsy N. Smalley, "Political Science: The Discipline, The Literature, and The Library," *Libri*, 30 (1980): 33-52; and Alice Robbin, "Strategies for Improving Utilization of Computerized Statistical Data by the Social Scientific Community," *Social Science Information Studies*, 1 (1981): 89-109.

31. Robbin, "Strategies for Improving Utilization," p. 90.

32. Vondran, "The Effect of Method of Research on the Information Seeking Behavior of Academic Historians," pp. 156-157.

33. Smalley, "Political Science," pp. 37-41.

34. Robbin, "Strategies for Improving Utilization."

35. Ibid., p. 97.

36. Ibid., p. 102.

37. For a summary of the effort to achieve bibliographic control over machine-readable files, *see* Sue A. Dodd, "Toward Integration of Catalog Records on Social Science Machine-Readable Data Files into Existing Bibliographic Utilities: A Commentary," *Library Trends*, 30 (Winter 1982): 335-36l.

38. For a detailed narrative of efforts to establish data libraries from 1957-1975, *see* Kathleen M. Heim, "Social Science Data Archives: A User Study," Ph. D. dissertation, University of Wisconsin-Madison, 1980.

39. For a discussion of the need to develop data library services, *see* Judith S. Rowe, "Expanding Social Science Reference Service to Meet the Needs of Patrons More Adequately," *Library Trends*, 30 (Winter 1982): 327-334.

40. Heim, "Social Science Data Archives," p. 173; Robbin, "Strategies for Improving Utilization," p. 100.

41. President's Reorganization Project, "Federal Statistical System: Access and Dissemination," in *Reanalyzing Program Evaluations: Policies and Practices for Secondary Analysis of Social and Educational Programs*," eds. Robert F. Boruch, Paul M. Wortman, and David S. Cordray (San Francisco: Jossey-Bass, 1981), pp. 21-33; Joseph W. Duncan, "Accessing Social Statistics," *Library Trends*, 30 (Winter 1982): 363-376.

42. J. Timothy Sprehe, "A Federal Policy for Improving Data Access and User Services," *Statistical Reporter*, (March 1981) pp. 323-341.

43. U.S. Department of Commerce, Office of Federal Statistical Policy and Standards, *A Framework for Planning U.S. Federal Statistics for the 1980's* (Washington, D.C.: G.P.O., 1978).

44. Sprehe, "A Federal Policy for Improving Data Access and User Services," p. 323.

45. Ibid.

46. Ibid., p. 324.

47. Ibid.

48. Ibid., p. 325.

49. Myra L. Triplett, "The Role of Interagency Committees in Statistical Policy Coordination." *Statistical Reporter* (October 1980) p. 1.

50. Sprehe, "A Federal Policy for Improving Data Access and User Services," p. 326.

51. Triplett, "The Role of Interagency Committees in Statistical Policy Coordination," p. 4-5.

52. Sprehe, "A Federal Policy for Improving Data Access and User Services," p. 327.

53. Ibid., p. 328.

54. Ibid., pp. 328-329.

55. Ibid.

56. Ibid., pp. 329-330.

57. Ibid., p. 330

58. Ibid., pp. 331-332.

59. Ibid., p. 333.

60. Ibid.

61. Ibid.

62. Ibid., pp. 334-335.

63. Ibid., p. 335.

64. Ibid., p. 336.

65. Ibid.

66. U.S. Department of Commerce, National Technical Information Service and Office of Federal Statistical Policy and Standards, *Directory of Federal Statistical Data Files*. Available from NTIS (order number: PB 81-133175).

67. Sprehe, "A Federal Policy for Improving Data Access and User Services," p. 338.

68. Ibid., pp. 338-339.

69. Ibid., p. 339.

70. Ibid.

71. Ibid., pp. 340-341. Concluding remarks, especially.

72. Barton M. Clark, "Social Science Data Archives and Libraries: A View to the Future," *Library Trends*, 30 (Winter 1982): 505-509.

73. Alice Robbin, "Technical Guidelines for Preparing and Documenting Data," in *Reanalyzing Program Evaluations: Policies and Practices for Secondary Analysis of Social and Educational Programs*, eds. Robert F. Boruch, Paul M. Wortman, and David S. Cordray (San Francisco: Jossey-Bass, 1981), p. 86.

74. Ibid.

75. Ibid., p. 87.

76. American Library Association, *Anglo-American Cataloging Rules*, 2nd, ed. (Chicago: American Library Association, 1978), pp. 201-216.

77. Dodd, "Toward Integration of Catalog Records on Social Science Machine-Readable Data Files into Existing Bibliographic Utilities."

78. U.S. Department of Commerce, NTIS and OFSPS.

79. "Federal Statistical Data File Catalogs and Directories," and "Selected Data Access Publications" *Statistical Reporter*, (March 1981) pp. 341-344.

80. Anthony T. Kruzas, *Encyclopedia of Information Systems and Services* (Detroit: Gale Research, 1980).

81. Paul Wasserman, *Statistics Sources*, 7th ed. (Detroit: Gale Research, 1982).

82. This service, originally called the Statistical Data Reference Service, is now known as Numbers Please. For information call DUALabs at 703-525-1480.

83. For information on IASSIST, *see* the *IASSIST Newsletter*.

84. The Association of Public Data Users publishes a newsletter and a directory of members' data-file holdings. APOUO: 1601 N. Kent State, Suite 900, Arlington, Virginia 22209

85. Alice Robbin, "The Pre-Acquisition Process: A Strategy for Locating and Acquiring Machine-Readable Data," *Drexel Library Quarterly*, 13 (January 1977): 21-42.

86. Howard D. White, "Social Science Data Sets: A Study for Librarians," Ph.D. dissertation, University of California, Berkeley, 1974.

87. Ray Jones, "The Data Library in the University of Florida Libraries, *Library Trends*, 30 (Winter 1982): 395.

88. Michael O'Hare, "Information Management and Public Choice," in *Research in Public Policy Analysis and Management: Basic Theory, Methods, and Perspectives*, ed. John P. Crecine (Greenwich, Conn.: JAI Press, 1981), p. 224.

89. Ibid., pp. 246-247.

90. The Association for Public Policy Analysis and Management publishes a series on methodological and theoretical issues in policy science; The National Research Council, Study Project on Social Research and Development, has released the following studies: *The Federal Investment in Knowledge of Social Problems; The Funding of Social Knowledge Production and Application; Studies in the Management of Social R & D; Knowledge and Policy*; and *The Uses of Basic Research*. The Organisation for Economic Co-operation and Development has published a book of case studies on this topic: *The Utilisation of the Social Sciences in Policy-Making in the United States* (Paris, OECD, 1980).

91. James H. Laue, "Sociology and the Just Society," in *Social Scientists as Advocates: Views from the Applied Disciplines*, ed. George H. Weber and George J. McCall (Beverly Hills: Sage, 1978), p. 167.

92. Ibid., p. 169.

GOVERNMENT MAP PUBLICATIONS: AN OVERVIEW

By Charles A. Seavey

Will Durant has said, "Let us look at the map, for maps, like faces, are the signatures of history."[1] Marshall McLuhan has written that without maps "the world of modern science and technologies would hardly exist."[2] Norman J.W. Thrower, Professor of Geography at UCLA, believes that "it is important for educated people to know about maps, even though they may not be called upon to make them."[3] Walter W. Ristow, long time chief of the Geography and Map Division, Library of Congress, and thereby head of the world's largest map collection, estimated that eighty percent of all maps are produced by government entities.[4] In preparing this chapter, the author has come to the conclusion that Dr. Ristow may even have understated the case.

The U.S. Geological Survey recently estimated that the federal government distributes 161,000,000 maps and charts annually.[5] In a federal warehouse in Denver, Colorado, 75,000,000 maps are stored, awaiting shipment to depositories or sale to the public, and new maps arrive there at the rate of 2½ *boxcar-loads* every month![6] A NASA survey indicates that total federal expenditures for mapping activities in the United States amount to $890,000,000 per fiscal year.[7] The amount spent by state and local agencies can only be surmised, but clearly we are not even talking about a minor portion of the taxpayers' money here.

Given the extent of the mapping activities, this chapter will attempt only a brief overview of a rather large subject. It will examine the historical development of map-making as a government activity, a number of governmentally produced cartographic products, access to the array of information, and a look at where we may be going. The agencies discussed will range from the United Nations to the Middle Rio Grande Council of Governments. The maps will cover areas as exotic as Mars and as ordinary as a neighborhood in Albuquerque. During the course of this overview, two themes will be developed: (1) the incredible variety of information that lends itself to spatial presentation, and (2) the relationship between government-produced maps and those published by commercial firms.

Historical Background

Maps have been in existence in one form or another in many cultures virtually since the idea of recording data occurred to our distant ancestors. Map development generally kept pace with the development of written language, although there are examples of maps being produced by cultures which had no written forms of expression. In the post-Roman Western world, maps, like written records, were largely the province of the Church. With the coming of the Renaissance and the rediscovery of Ptolemy, map-making entered a new and vigorous period as a commercial venture. The great Italian, Dutch, French, and English map-makers were all part of what we now call the private sector. In the eighteenth century, however, two fundamental changes took place in France, and these involved one family of map-makers.

The Cassini family was the first to produce a modern map—modern in the sense that it was a large-scale, multi-sheet, quadrangle-formatted map based on triangulation and trigonometric survey. The Cassini Survey also was the first map-making operation with substantial, if intermittent, government support. Revolutionary and Imperial France recognized the value of these maps, and continued to support their production. The Cassini Surveys eventually became the basis of the Institut Geographique National, the official mapping agency of France.

At the turn of the eighteenth century, other nations adopted map-making as an official function. Britain's Ordnance Survey was formed in 1790, and other European nations followed suit.

In the United States government mapping started during the Revolutionary War and has never stopped since. As a young federal government acquired more and more of the vast continent, mapping activities took two paths. The first path was basically one of exploration and reconnaissance, largely administered by the Army. Lewis and Clark, John C. Fremont, J.C. Ives, and G.K. Warren were all either in, or closely connected to, the Army during the first two-thirds of the nineteenth century. The second path was the less romantic task of measuring public lands into one-mile squares to help finance the westward move.[8]

The early nation was heavily dependent upon sea-borne commerce, and the Coastal Survey started producing coastal nautical charts in 1807, while the Navy started charting deep water areas in the 1830s. In conjunction with Army and General Land Office activities, these efforts marked the beginnings of federal mapping.

The maps of surveyors and explorers were adequate for their time, but much more detail was needed for proper exploitation of the mineral wealth of the nation. To meet this need, the U.S. Geological Survey (USGS) was formed in 1879 and soon commenced the task of producing large-scale topographic maps of the country—a job they promise will be complete by the end of *this* decade! After the formation of USGS, other agencies started appearing and producing maps at public expense: the Forest Service, the Bureau of Mines, etc. World War II brought the military back into the mapping business on a large scale, when the Defense Mapping Agency was hastily formed.

Government mapping, therefore, is not a recent phenomenon. The pattern of government involvement in mapping is by no means unique to the U.S., France, and Britain. The U.S. Geological Survey's *Worldwide Directory of National Earth Science Agencies and Related International Organizations* is over 80 pages long and lists the official mapping agencies of over 160 nations. It also covers 87 international organizations concerned in some way with earth science or mapping.[9]

Government-Produced Cartographic Products

Today many international organizations directly produce, or cooperate in the production of, maps and charts. The U.N. produces many maps, such as the *Geologic Map of the World* and the *Metamorphic Map of Africa*. Nautical charts, which are produced through international cooperation, often involve the U.S. Defense Mapping Agency and various international mapping agencies such as the British Hydrographic Office, the coordination of which is handled through an office in Monaco. A famous example of international cooperation is the *International Map of the World (IMW)*. First proposed in the 1890s, the idea was to create a map of the entire world, produced to a uniform set of specifications, with each nation responsible for mapping its own territory. The project was initiated officially in 1913, which, as it turned out, was not a particularly good year in which to undertake international cooperative ventures. The result was that the *IMW* never really got off the ground in the manner envisioned by its original proponents. It has also resulted in some ironic situations. In 1940 the British in North Africa were doubtless using an Anglo-French map produced to *IMW* specifications for planning their struggle against Rommel. Rommel, for his part, was using German maps produced to the same set of specifications, often using the same sources, and carrying the same title. While many nations have not had new *IMW* mapping for thirty or forty years, others have made good use of the format to produce some exceptionally fine modern maps.[10]

National mapping agencies, particularly those of the United States, often produce maps of places that are not easily accessible. Early USAF and NASA maps of the Moon, for example, have been used by commercial map-makers as the basis for cartographic products of a planetary satellite that they themselves could not hope to visit. The same pattern has been repeated with governmentally produced maps of Mars, and the government is now working on producing maps of Mercury. Can commercial cartography be far behind?[11]

Moving from the exotic to the more ordinary, various agencies produce maps of the earth. One such map, the Defense Mapping Agency's series 1142 map of the world, is a superb example of the relationship between government and commercial cartography. This series was originally compiled by the American Geographical Society (a private scholarly organization) in the 1930s. The AGS cartographers used as their source the official maps of a number of countries. In 1949 the Army Map Service took over the service from the AGS. The 1142 series, as it is called, is now sold by the Defense Mapping Agency.[12]

To more fully illustrate the wide subject range of governmentally produced maps, let us take a trip through the subject divisions of the "G" Classification Schedule of the Library of Congress. "G" is probably the classification scheme most widely used for map collections in this country. The main subject breakdowns are as follows (examples of each subject are drawn from the map collection of the University of New Mexico):*

A. Special Category Maps and Atlases.
    A1. Outline and base maps.
        Outline map of the United States. 1:17m, 1972. NOAA.
        Base Map. 1:3m, 1965. USGS.
    A4. Photomaps.
        Conterminous U.S. Satellite Image. 1:5m, n.d. USGS/NASA.
B. Mathematical Geography...aspects of cartography, surveying and mapping.

----

*The conference presentation was based on a slide set developed by the author.

B5. Surveying, extent of areas surveyed or mapped.
   Topographic Mapping Status. 1:3m, 1979. USGS.
C. Physical Sciences. Distribution of natural phenomena of the earth, the atmosphere and subsurface features.
   C1. General.
      United States 1:7m, ca. 1900. USGS (the Gannett Map) shows relief, hydrology and stylized bathymetry. OVERALL DETAIL OF THE SAME MAP. SW CORNER.

Series of USGS Topographic Maps

"The Simple Topographic Map" is in reality a very complex concentration of information showing the "phenomena of the earth," which, when you think about it, is a pretty awesome task. This chapter mentions a few simple 1:24,000 topo maps to demonstrate some of the features, both natural and artificial, that can be studied on a map.

Vantage, Oregon

In one small area, there are political boundaries, land survey boundaries, a river, rail and highway lines, a dam, a bridge, powerlines, individual houses, forested areas, some fairly sharp relief, bathymetric data (fishermen love it), an orchard, drainage ditches a radio tower, etc. This is what I think of as a border or transitional area between man and his environment—neither one truly dominating.

Cumberland, Maryland

This map introduces two new concepts: built up areas, shown in pink, and photorevisions, shown in purple. Between published editions of the map (1949 and 1979) a highway has been built; buildings have been enlarged and new ones constructed; a whole new area has been added to the built-up category; and parts of the hillsides have been dug away by mining. Again, a transitional area, although evidence of man is much heavier than in the previous map.

Convington, Kentucky

On a topo sheet, several categories of public buildings (schools, libraries, churches, etc.) are identified by shape. Railyards, a sewage disposal plant, and Three Rivers Stadium are all clearly visible. As is evident, this is an area dominated by the cultural (i.e., the man-made), rather than the natural landscape.

Santa Rita Bridge, California

This is a fairly simple area consisting of a maze of drainage ditches, and streams of various sizes. There is very little in the way of elevation to depict; however, this map is built to the same general specifications as the previous three. The topographic map is clearly "general purpose" only in the sense that it serves a multiplicity of functions.

Rozel Point SW, Utah

Of course, sometimes a map really does exist for just one purpose. This map shows absolutely *nothing* other than a blue color and the words "Great Salt Lake." It exists only to be mosaicked with surrounding maps to make a larger map of Salt Lake City. If this map did not exist, there would be a large rectangular hole in the middle of the larger map.

The Geological Survey has been working on producing topo maps of the country for just about one hundred years. Over those years there have been a number of format changes and a steady increase in the size of the scale that was considered standard. Old editions of topos are just as valuable in their way as the current ones. The "old" map is a picture of a time that no longer is. Furthermore, it is an *accurate* picture of that time, which can convey information that no written description possibly could. Let us take a look at the history of the city of Albuquerque, New Mexico, as shown in the various topographic maps that cover the area:

1893 (1:125,000) Bernallio Quadrangle

This was quite literally the wild West. The Rio Grande flows untouched and undirected by human hands. Albuquerque consists of a very few square blocks in the midst of miles and miles of open space.

1937 (1:62,500) Albuquerque Quadrangle

The city has started to move up out of the valley and into the "heights." The road pattern is rather more complex (Route 66 bridges the river), and the public surveys have halted rather abruptly at the boundary of an old Spanish land-grant.

1954 (1:24,000) Los Griegos Quadrangle

Yet another increase in scale, so now we concentrate on an area in the northwest part of the city rather than the whole area. Drainage ditches have appeared along the Rio Grande, and many more houses are in evidence. The city has started its post-war boom period.

1960 (1:24,000) Los Griegos Quadrangle

Six years later there are fewer orchards, but the built up area has increased dramatically. New drainage ditches have appeared on the east side of the river, and at least two new schools have been built. Life is becoming more complex.

1967 (1:24K, photorevision) Los Griegos Quadrangle

The purple areas show new buildings, and new areas being tracted for housing in the northwest heights.

1972 (1:24K, photorevision) Los Griegos Quadrangle

A whole new "townhouse" complex has appeared on the west bank of the river, and the city continues to fill in.

This has been a very sketchy trip through seventy-nine years of the history of one location. Some cities have accumulated more maps over a similar time period, while others have not. Nonetheless, the maps for any municipality over time will show similar kinds of changes. After all, areas are not re-mapped if there has been little change.

This chapter has focused on topo maps for two reasons. First, no other map depicts so much data for so many different purposes. Second, this type of map forms the vast bulk of virtually every map collection in this (or any) country. It takes over 57,000 1:24K quads to cover the continental United States. Virtually every other country has an equivalent series of maps. Knowledge of what a topo is, and what it can tell you, is an important way of tapping into government information.

Class C, Physical Sciences (continued):
　　C2. Physiography, Geomorphology.
　　　　United States, shaded relief. 1:7.5m. USGS. This map, incidentally, was drawn by Richard Edes Harrison, whose maps graced the pages of *Life* and *Look* for many years, particularly during World War II.
　　C3. Hydrology/Hydrogeology.
　　　　Water Surplus and Water Deficiency in the United States. 1965. USGS.
　　C5. Geology.
　　　　Geologic Map of the United States (western half). 1975. USGS.

D. Biogeography. Maps depicting the distribution of plant and animal life.
  D1. General.
    Ecoregions of the United States. 1979. Forest Service.
  D5. Wildlife conservation and reserves or refuges.
    National Wildlife Refuge System. 1:3,168,000. 1979. Fish & Wildlife
    Service.
E. Human and Cultural Geography. Anthropogeography. Human Ecology.
  E1. General, including ethnology, tribes, ethnic groups, etc.
    Indian Land Areas. 1:5m. 1971. Indian Affairs Bureau.
  E2. Population. There are probably as many ways of depicting popu-
    lation as any single subject that can be mapped. Simple headcount
    can be shown with great elegance:
    Population Distribution, Urban and Rural, in the United States. 1970.
    (Census Bureau) wherein one segment of the population may be
    singled out and highlighted, e.g.:
    Number of American Indians, by counties of the United States, 1970, or
    another variable can be added to a rather more complex map,
    e.g.,
    *Distribution of Older Americans in 1970 Related to Year of Maximum
    County Population*. Census Bureau.
    The GE-50 series of population maps put out by the Census Bu-
    reau can possibly tell you more about population trends in a
    shorter time than any other medium.
  E6. Social and Cultural Geography.
    Rural Cultural Regions of the United States. 1940. Agriculture Dept/WPA.
  E63. Recreation and Sports (hiking, camping, hunting, fishing, etc.).
    The National Park System. 1980. National Park Service.
F. Political Geography. Maps on boundaries, political divisions. . . etc.
  F7. Administrative and Political Divisions.
    State and County Boundaries, 1960. Census Bureau.
  F9. Political Campaigns, Election results.
    Presidential Elections and Political Parties, 1789- (from the National
    Atlas).
G. Economic Geography.
  G17. Economic Assistance (Domestic).
    Economic Development Districts. 1:7.5m. 1978. Economic Develop-
    ment Administration.
  G4. Land, land use, land capabilities and classification.
    Index to Land Use Maps. 1978. USGS.
    Land Resource Regions. 1965. Soil Conservation Service.
  G5. Public Lands.
    United States of America. 1:3m. 1964. USGS. This is one of the most
    versatile maps published by the USGS. A slightly later edition

shows the public land surveys. That version, or this one, could just as easily have been classed in S (history), G4, F, and possibly one or two more categories.

H. Mines and Mineral Resources.
  H8. Petroleum and Gas.
    Oil and Gas Fields of the United States (east half). 1964. USGS.
  H9. Coal.
    Coal Fields of the United States. 1960. USGS.
J. Agriculture.
  J3. Soils and Soil Classification.
    Soil Survey of the United States. 1931. Agriculture Dept.
K. Forests and Forestry.
  K2. Distribution of Forest Areas and types...
    Forest and Range Ecosystems. 1974. Forest Service.
L. Aquatic Biological Resources.
  L2. Fishing and Fisheries.
    Commercial Fishing. From the National Atlas.
M. Manufacturing and Processing.
  M2. Mineral Processing and Manufacture.
    Primary Metal Industries. From the National Atlas.
N. Technology, Engineering, Public Works.
  N3. Power.
  N32. *Geothermal Energy in the Western United States.* 1978. NOAA.
  N4. Electric Utilities and Power Lines.
    Major Extra High Voltage Lines, 1978. DOE.
P. Transportation and Communication.
  P2. Roads.
    National System of Interstate and Defense Highways. 1977. Federal Highway Administration.
  P3. Railroads.
    Amtrak's Nationwide Passenger System. 1980. AMTRAK.
  P4. Pipelines.
    Major Natural Gas Pipelines, 1980. DOE.
  P5. Water Transportation.
    Point Sur to San Francisco. NOAA medium-scale Nautical Chart.
    San Francisco Bay. NOAA large-scale Nautical Chart.
    Existing Waterways and Ports. 1:7.5m. 1979. USGS.
  P6. Air Transport.
    ONC. 1:,000,000 covering part of the Eastern Seaboard. Airplane pilots use a map very similar to this. When they get close to Washington, D.C., they turn to the *Washington Sectional Aeronautical Chart,* 1:500,000 cover showing index to maps of the whole country.

Detail of Washington SAC. An aerial view of Washington, D.C. Thematic: *United States Air Transportation System...* 1969. Civil Aeronautics Board.
Q. Commerce and Trade. Finance.
  Q3. Movement of Commodities.
      Total Commodity Movement by Water, 1976. USGS.
  Q8. Finance.
      Structure of Commercial Banking. 1970. Federal Reserve.
R. Military and Naval Geography.
  R2. Military and naval districts and establishments.
      Major Army, Navy, and Air Force Installations in the United States. 1979.
DMA *Detail of the Same Map.*
S. Historical Geography.   On this subject the government has some real advantages. Most of the time it either made the original maps (as in the example of *Civil War Maps*—folio published by the National Ocean Survey, 1965) and can do a good job of reproduction and explanation, or government officials *used* the map. In the latter case, they sometimes do a bad job of reproduction, as in this rather ghastly example: *Mitchell/Franklin* (reproduced by the Constitutional Sesquicentennial Commission). This 1782 map by John Mitchell, which appeared in the *American State Papers*, was the standard map used in the Anglo-American peace negotiations leading to the Treaty of Paris. A version of it was apparently modified by Benjamin Franklin. In any kind of decent reproduction it is a striking and accurate map.

Government maps can also show the metamorphosis of government agencies. For example, *Roberdeau, 1818* (reproduced by the Army Corps of Engineers) is a map of the eastern two-thirds of what later became the United States. It was originally done by the Topographical Bureau, which would become the Corps of Topographical Engineers and eventually part of the Corps of Engineers as it is known today.

Similar patterns are evident when one examines the maps produced by state and local agencies. The overall cartographic rendering, however, gets slightly less elegant at the state level. There are maps similar to those produced federally, but a higher proportion of the maps are made for in-house use and tend to be produced by monochromatic processes on cheap paper. At local levels of government, maps get pretty utilitarian, but are just as valuable.[13]

Access to Government Cartographic Information

If you think access to printed government documents is less than ideal, access to government *maps* is several cuts below that. Actually accessibility to maps ranges from fairly good to nearly impossible. The "standard" maps dealing with land, air, and water are all widely understood and relatively easy to find. A library does not need to have a huge map collection in order to own topo sheets covering the local area, or a set of aeronautical charts, or local nautical charts (depending on location). Once you are aware of their existence, USGS topo sheets can be located through the use of index maps and are generally filed alphabetically. This is unsophisticated, but effective. Variations of this theme work for virtually all quadrangle-based maps, no matter who produces them. Aeronautical and nautical charts also employ the index map system. Although most of us are more or less cartographically illiterate, most people pick up the system fairly quickly.

Beyond the standard products, the picture darkens considerably. Within the library world, maps, with a few notable exceptions, are treated as third or fourth class citizens. There are a number of reasons for this treatment. Some are simply societal in nature, while others are more specific to the field of librarianship.

First, as mentioned above, this is a cartographically illiterate nation. The maps that school children must deal with, all the way through high school, are of the "Dick and Jane" variety. Although my experience with children convinces me that they are able to deal with fairly sophisticated cartographic concepts, in school they get outline maps (in which Greenland is twice as big as South America) and not much else. At home, if they are lucky, they are exposed to National Geographic maps, which, unfortunately, are not much more complex than the maps and atlases they see at school. Maps in the newspapers and on television for the most part are of the same sort: simple outline maps. Eventually the children grow up; some become school teachers; and the cycle resumes. Children rapidly graduate from "Dick and Jane" in their reading skills, and the school system goes to great lengths to nurture their progress. Some serious research on what children can and cannot understand in this area needs to be done. There is no reason that primary and secondary cartographic interpretation skills cannot be taught alongside (and at the same pace) as reading skills.

Second, maps have been regarded as "cheap" by most of us for a long time. Perhaps each of us remembers a book collection in our childhood home. The books are neatly stacked, dusted occasionally, and guarded from harm (my mother had a heavy hand if one of us mistreated a book, and the howls of a dog that had the temerity actually to chew on one still ring in my memory). Contrast this with your experience of maps. The local gas station *gave* them away. Your father kept a pile in the glove compartment of the car. After a while they would get torn, smeared with ice cream, make their way to that pile of detritus under the seat, and eventually be thrown away and replaced with new ones. A mind set had been created there: maps are simple things that may be thoughtlessly discarded—they are not important!

Within the library world, maps have a mixed history. Some institutions have placed a fair amount of emphasis at least on acquiring them, while others have ignored them completely. There is no apparent pattern to which libraries do and which do not collect maps. *Map Collections in the United States and Canada* (3rd ed., 1978) identifies 684 U.S. map collections. Of these, 345 are identifiable as being in academic institutions. Since there are over 1,900 four-year institutions of higher learning in the U.S., only a small percentage of institutions collect maps.[14] We need a thorough analysis of why some institutions have map collections numbering in the hundreds of thousands, while others ignore them entirely.

Bibliographic access to maps is even more confused than their presence of lack thereof. There has never been a generally accepted system of cataloging and classifying maps. Hence the full attention of the library profession has never focused on developing bibliographic control and access to maps the way it has on books and government documents. Two factors seem to be at work in this matter.

Prior to 1900, maps and books were roughly in the same position in terms of bibliographic control. Then, in 1904, Phillip Lee Phillips, then head of the map collection of the Library of Congress, ventured that he did not see any reason why maps should not be cataloged in the same way as books.[15] In the days when main entry was a major access point, this meant that maps were first cataloged by their "responsible authority," completely ignoring the fact that virtually all users are interested primarily in the *area* a map covers, and only secondarily in the responsible authority. The regrettable, albeit predictable, result of Phillips' statement was that most libraries simply went their own way and devised some area-based system of access. By 1967 a noted Canadian map librarian could state that "there are probably as many individual map cataloging and classification schemes in the world as there are map libraries."[16] As late as 1977 this author had to devise his own system for cataloging a university map collection, simply because the LC/AACR I practice was time-consuming and, in a number of ways, totally unproductive in a user-oriented environment.[17]

Theoretically the advent of computer-assisted shared cataloging networks should put an end to this chaotic situation, and to an extent it has. This author seriously doubts that anybody now starting to catalog a collection would use anything but LC/AACR2 practice. Certainly had OCLC been available in 1977, this author would not have devised the system he did.

And yet, we are still not taking full advantage of the computer's capabilities. We are, by and large, simply using the computer as a printing device for a bibliographic format that has existed for years, and are following rules that have not changed *fundamentally* since library cards were done in script. We are still required to spend enormous amounts of time on descriptive cataloging and authority work. While a certain amount of descriptive cataloging is necessary, authority work, particularly for government documents and maps, is a waste or misuse of time. In an age when OCLC, the largest of the bibliographic utilities, has just added its eight millionth record, we are still using a subject access system that was first published in 1910![18] We are still trying to follow Phillip Lee Phillips and apply book cataloging practice to maps.

Although RLIN and WLN have more sophisticated search techniques, OCLC can still offer nothing better than title searches. With an incredible number of maps titled "Map of the . . . ," it is a losing proposition. If OCLC could add a search key for the 052 field (map classification number— essentially the LC "G" class number) the situation would improve dramatically. In the meantime, the advent of shared cataloging networks has not dramatically improved access to cartographic information.

The second factor hampering bibliographic access to maps is essentially a political one. The map library profession has always been a small one, and prior to 1944 it had no organized voice within the library profession. In that year the Geography and Map Division was organized as part of the Special Libraries Association.[19] While the G&M Division did create a certain unity among full-time map librarians, and continues to produce an excellent quarterly *Bulletin*, it also had the effect of separating map librarians from the mainstream of the library world. One result is that, by and large, the literature of map librianship was read only by those already "in the know." A whole generation of library administrators has grown up largely unaware of the potential (and problems) of the map format. Second, map librarians had no active voice in decisions made by the American Library Association. Suffice it to say, the word "map" does not exist in *any* of ALA's standards for various types of libraries.[20]

Where does this leave us in terms of access to governmentally produced maps? Federally produced maps are at least being entered into machine-readable format, even if the largest bibliographic utility is singularly ill-designed to make use of it. The "standard" maps, once one locates a collection, are easily found. For everything else, users are by and large dependent upon the skill and knowledge of the mapkeeper. And here a third inhibiting factor appears.

Traditional library education has not been particularly helpful in training librarians with the map format. The gentleman who taught my government publications course made the effort of bringing in a map librarian (which is perhaps more than most do); but one hour was a woefully inadequate time in which to come to grips with a very complex format. If library schools cannot see their way clear to offering a course in maps and map librarianship every now and then (and a few do), then they should at least try to work the material into other courses. Basic reference and cataloging courses, bibliography of the social and physical sciences; these types of library courses all lend themselves to some small bits of training with the cartographic format. Certainly the government documents course looks like an ideal place to build in some more time with maps. Painful though the experience may be, library educators, if they have not already done so, might read Mary Larsgaard's recent article.[21]

Access to state and locally produced maps is very much a question of luck. At the state level, some are better than others. Illinois has a state map information center operating out of the Map and Geography collection at the University of Illinois, Champaign-Urbana. Other states with large *modern* map collections probably provide good access to their own products. Arizona, Kansas, and Wisconsin spring immediately to mind in this category.

County and locally produced maps are probably hopeless for anything other than strictly local situations. Except for obvious things like bus routes and tourist-oriented material, most agencies at this level are producing maps largely for internal use and do not understand why anybody else would want them.There is virtually no bibliographic control over any of this material, and much less effort at acquisition on the part of libraries and archives. A great deal of the cartographic history of the nation probably gets discarded every time a new city hall gets built and all the "old stuff" is thrown away. All librarians need to be more alert to the important collections of local material that may become available in this way.

The Future

Having painted a fairly depressing picture, this author can still look ahead with some optimism. The federal government is taking tentative steps toward some tighter coordination of its mapping activities. The Geological Survey recently reorganized and created a National Mapping Division, and the National Cartographic Information Center may eventually provide far better on-line access than is currently available. There is now an organized voice within the American Library Association. Although the Map and Geography Roundtable (MAGERT) is very new and very small, it has before it the incredibly successful Government Documents Roundtable as a role-model. Bernadine Hoduski, in the first chapter of this book, has made the point that political activism can be successful. Think back to what access to government documents was *before* the creation of GODORT, and compare it to today. This will give you an idea of what might well happen for the cartographic format. Although MAGERT is starting from a weaker position than GODORT did, a lot of ice has been broken, and precedents have been set.

If the library world does not soon learn how to handle maps, it is going to miss out on a lot. There have been two major revolutions in map-making over the years. The first was the introduction, by the Cassinis, of the mathematical basis of the work. The second was the introduction of aerial photography in the 1920s and 1930s. Aerial photography, and the later satellite imagery, have profoundly affected the way maps are made. The third revolution, in the form of the computer, is now upon us. Here, this author is not referring only to access to maps, but to the actual design and production of cartographically formatted information. Kathleen Heim, in another chapter of this book, discusses DIDS and DADS, but that is just the tip of the iceberg. The traditional printed map, as we know it, will eventually be replaced by a computer-generated and printed "map-on-demand" system capable of generating (in hours or minutes rather than years) maps showing a complex mix of variables. The U.S. Geological Survey is in the process of converting its topographic data base into machine-readable format. Around nine hundred quadrangles have been converted already, and the project goes on.[22] The quadrangle maps will eventually be stored, recalled, and updated online, and hardcopy maps will be produced on demand. Combining this data base with the vast amount of socioeconomic data already in machine-readable form is but a few steps beyond.

At the moment, of course, these advances are made possible only by the expenditure of a *lot* of money. If the trend toward minaturization and the decreasing cost of hardware continues, however, this author can expect to convert a university map collection to a computer operation within the next ten years. Remember, yesterday's UNIVAC is today's Apple II, and goodness knows what will happen tomorrow!

This chapter has been a reconnaissance of the world of governmentally produced maps—their information value, and some of their problems and possibilities. This author does not expect all readers to become zealous converts to the format, but he does suggest that libraries and information-transfer specialists can make far better use of maps than they have in the past.

References

1. Will Durant and Ariel Durant, *The Story of Civilization, Part VII:The Age of Reason Begins...* (New York: Simon and Schuster, 1961), p. 495.

2. Marshall McLuhan, *Understanding Media* (New York: McGraw-Hill, 1964), p. 157.

3. Norman J. W. Thrower, *Maps and Man* (Englewood Cliffs, N.J.: Prentice-Hall, 1972), p.1.

4. Walter W. Ristow, "The Emergence of Maps in Libraries," *Special Libraries*, 58, no. 6 (July-August 1967): 402.

5. William A. Radlinski, "Federal Mapping and Charting in the United States." Paper presented at the 9th International Conference on Cartography, 26 July 1978, University of Maryland, College Park.

6. Information presented by Dwight Canfield (Center Director) during a tour of the U.S. Geological Survey Distribution Center, Denver, CO, 11 February 1982.

7. Electrostatic copy of a portion of an unpublished 1981 (?) NASA report in this writer's possession.

8. This background material is drawn from a number of sources and has been incorporated in several articles by this author, the most recent of which is "Collection Development for Government Map Collections," *Government Publications Review*, 8A (1981): 17-20.

9. *Worldwide Directory of National Earth Science Agencies and Related International Organizations*, U.S. Geological Survey Circular 834 (Reston, VA: the Survey, 1981).

10. Slides included:

a. United Nations, *Geologic World Atlas*, sheet 2, 1:10,000,000 (1974).

b. *Metamorphic Map of Africa*, 1:10,000,000 (1978).

c. Defense Mapping Agency, *North Atlantic Ocean*, 1:10,000,000, International (Nautical) Chart Series INT 14 (1975).

d. Defense Mapping Agency, *Northeast Coast of South America*, 1:3,500,000, International (Nautical) Chart Series INT 107 (1975).

e. *International Map of the World at 1:1,000,000*, data sheet or legend, (ca. 1913).

f. *International Map of the World at 1:1,000,000, Erg Chech*, sheet NG-30 (1940).

g. *International Map of the World at 1:1,000,000, Erg Schesch*, sheet NG-30 (1940).

h. *International Map of the World at 1:1,000,000, Meekatharra*, sheet SG-50 (1971).

11. Slides included:

a. U.S. Air Force, *Lunar Image Mosaic*, LEM-1, 1:5,000,000 (1962).

b. Army Map Service, *Mare Nectaris—Mare Ibrium*, 1:2,500,000 (1962).

c. U.S. Geological Survey, *Geologic Map of the Julius Caesar Quadrangle of the Moon*, map I- 510, 1:1,000,000 (1967).

d. U.S. Geological Survey, *Index Map of the Subterrestrial Hemisphere of the Moon* (n.d.).

e. National Geographic Society. *The Earth's Moon*. 1976.

f. U.S. Geological Survey, *Cartographic Atlas of Mars: Tharsis Quadrangle*, map I-926, 1:5,000,000 (1976).

g. National Geographic Society, *The Red Planet Mars* (1973).

h. U.S. Geological Survey, *Shaded Relief Map of the Michelangelo Quadrangle of Mercury*, map I-1067 (1977).

12. Slides included:

a. Defense Mapping Agency, *The World*, series 1142, sheet 5, 1:11,000,000 (1971).

b. Defense Mapping Agency, *The World*, series 1106, sheet 11, 1:5,000,000 (1963).

13. Slides included:

a. New Mexico State Highway Department, *State of New Mexico* (highway map), 1:360,160 (1956).

b. New Mexico State Planning Office, *Critical Area Studies Maps: Slope, Santa Fe Quadrangle*, 1:250,000 (1980).

c. New Mexico State Library, *New Mexico Depository Libraries*, 1:1,000,000 (1981).

d. Middle Rio Grande Council of Governments, *Area Planning Jurisdiction No. 1* (1978?).

14. U.S. National Center for Education Statistics, *Education Statistics: Colleges and Universities, 1979-1980* (Washington: GPO, 1981), table 2, p. xxix.

15. Phillip Lee Phillips, "Maps and Atlases." In: Charles Ammi Cutter, *Rules for a Dictionary Catalog, Special Report on Public Libraries, Part II.* 4th ed. (U.S. Bureau of Education, 1904), p. 140.

16. Joan Winearls, "Some Problems in Classifying and Cataloging Maps" *Proceedings of the Association of Canadian Map Libraries* (1967), pp. 27-32.

17. University of Northern Iowa, *Map Collection Manual* (1979). The system uses LC "G" Schedule call numbers, with area main entries derived from the same source. The LC subject cutters are ignored in favor of using the subject heading list devised by the American Geographical Society.

18. Library of Congress, *Subject Headings*, 1st ed. (Washington, D.C.: The Library, 1909-1914).

19. Walter W. Ristow, *The Emergence of Maps in Libraries* (Hamden, CT: Linnet Books, 1980), p. 7.

20. Charles A. Seavey, "Developing the Academic Map Collection." Paper presented at the ACRL National Conference, Minneapolis, MN, October 1981, pp. 4-5.

21. Mary Larsgaard, "Education for Map Librarianship," *Library Trends*, 29, no. 3 (Winter 1981): 499-511.

22. Conversation with Gary North, Chief of Information and Data Services, U.S. Geological Survey, 26 March 1982.

WHITE MAN SPEAKS WITH FORKED TONGUE: AMERICAN INDIAN DISCONTENT WITH GOVERNMENT REPORTS

By Michael L. Tate

St. Paul, Minnesota was ablaze with the spirit of celebration, for the mighty Northern Pacific Railroad had been completed a short time earlier, and the vast stretches of land from Minnesota to the Pacific Northwest had been linked by a ribbon of iron. Now, in mid-September of 1883, politicians, railroad executives and pioneer families assembled in St. Paul for the official dedication of this engineering feat. Yet amid the celebrants was one strangely incongruous figure, the full-blood Hunkpapa Sioux leader Sitting Bull, who was barely seven years removed from the great Indian victory at the Little Big Horn. It was precisely because of his conspicuous role in that battle that Sitting Bull was invited to appear at this national event. Falsely labeled as "the killer of Custer," Sitting Bull was supposed to symbolically represent the "tamed Indian" who had left the primitive life of the war trail and accepted the progressive ways of his former adversaries.

A young army officer, who had been detailed to accompany the famous Indian chief from Standing Rock Reservation to St. Paul, drafted a short speech for his ward to present at the gathering. The carefully prepared words lauded the white man's technology and praised especially the Northern Pacific Railroad for bringing civilization to the peoples of the Great Plains. Following a number of routine speeches by other notables, Sitting Bull stepped forward to give his memorized remarks in the Lakota language, which would then be translated by an army interpreter. To the young soldier's horror, Sitting Bull presented an entirely different speech, a speech from the heart: "I hate you. I hate you. I hate all the white people. You are thieves and liars. You have taken away our land and made us outcasts, so I hate you...." The translator, maintaining his wits in a potentially explosive situation, presented the original version of the speech in English, and the audience reciprocated with warm applause, none the wiser to the trick this Sioux chief had attempted to play on them.[1]

Sitting Bull's declaration of almost a century ago closely parallels the problem that Indian peoples face even today—Whites, not Indians, speak (and make policy) for Native Americans. Although the full tragedy of Indian-White relations goes far beyond anything this short chapter can convey, a number of points can be raised about the veracity of government reports on Indian affairs. This is not merely an exercise in academic nit-picking, but a brief exposé of how federal documents become the cornerstone for policy. Stated quite simply, *fraudulent and misleading conclusions made in "sacrosanct" government reports sometimes form the basis of pernicious legislation.* While it is true that the rising Indian activism of the 1970s helped Native peoples gain more public attention to their viewpoints, major problems persist in the recording of those viewpoints. Thus, before the interested citizen becomes too complacent about the quality of future Indian-White relations, he or she should consider the pessimistic words of Sioux balladeer Floyd Westerman. He describes the hated Task Forces which still provide the basic materials for federal publications and policies:

> Let's send a task force down from Washington
>   and check out the complaints.
> The Indians are unhappy and
>   they're putting on paint.
> They say their treatment is not fair
>   and they blame the BIA.
> But you know you can't believe a single word
>   the redskins say.
>
> It's the very same old problems that
>   we had two years ago.
> They want more programs started, and the
>   funds are getting low.
> We'll go down and ask some questions
>   and just stand around awhile.
> Then we'll make out our reports, that we
>   can later file—

But it's got to be kept secret,
    no one should know we're there.
Let's send a task force down from Washington
    and check out the complaints.
The Indians are unhappy, but is there a time
    when they ain't?

Even though one may acknowledge that Westerman's charges are overstated, the truth remains that Indians generally distrust documents bearing the stamp of government approval. To illustrate this point more clearly, this chapter will briefly examine two printed byproducts of earlier government investigations and indicate how their misunderstandings helped create pernicious legislation. Second, this chapter will identify the currency of this problem by demonstrating its presence in recent federal publications and Bureau of Indian Affairs research procedures. Finally, it will point out a few of the more encouraging signs indicating that some recent government publications are approaching the subject in a more candid and honest way.

Two Historical Problems—The 1867 Doolittle Report and the 1928 Meriam Report

Ironically, the story began on a very promising note. In January 1867, a congressionally mandated task force submitted its final report entitled *Condition of the Indian Tribes*, or, as it came to be known, the "Doolittle Committee Report" (named in honor of the Wisconsin senator who directed it).[2] Intended as the most honest and encompassing appraisal of reservation conditions ever amassed in the nineteenth century, the report emerged from almost two years of grass-roots investigations. Senator Doolittle and his staff traveled throughout the West to collect information from agents, army officers and territorial politicians. Most important, however, was the absence of the Indian voice in this massive report. Clearly the field investigators had demonstrated the classic ethnocentric bias reflected in the reports of all nineteenth century government factfinders. They based their studies upon the premise that only White "experts" could properly assess the situation. Certainly Indians, with their narrow exposure to the outside world, could only think in terms of the old days of the buffalo hunt and the warrior societies, and would not be able to offer unbiased appraisals of reservation life. Or so thought the "experts."[3]

Equally distressing was the partisan nature of the Doolittle Report. Rather than examining specific Indian complaints and looking for more realistic methods of bridging the two cultures, the Commission members directed most of their criticisms at specific agents and former Commissioners of Indian Affairs. While in some cases the criticisms were warranted, much of it was groundless, based on unsubstantiated innuendo and vengeful motives. Committee member James W. Nesmith even went so far as to admit that his so-called "evidence" against former Commissioner William P. Dole was completely fabricated; but his venomous tirade was published in the final draft of the Doolittle Report anyway.[4]

The one-dimensional conclusion that emerged from this seminal study was the naive belief that simply by purging the Indian Service of corruption, a successful relationship between the red man and the white man could easily be established. Such a simplistic solution was fraught with danger because it implied that Indians would willingly give up their traditional ways if only proper White role models were provided for them to follow. Nothing in this highly regarded report honestly appraised the collective desire of Native Americans to maintain their cultures and resist the assimilationist goals of White reformers.

The four major recommendations of the Doolittle Report not only received considerable attention in Washington, they became part of official legislation during the following two decades. First, the call for an inspection system to eliminate corruption within the Indian Bureau led to the creation in 1869 of the Board of Indian Commissioners, which would exercise this watchdog capacity until 1933. Second, the conclusion that Indians faced extinction if they stood in the way of the White advance, led to such an expansion of the reservation system that within a decade virtually all tribesmen were assigned to agencies and prosecuted if they refused to remain. Third, the report's endorsement of continued Interior Department control over Indian affairs not only alienated the War Department, it also indirectly sanctioned the use of missionaries as agents. Indeed, President Ulysses S. Grant's "Peace Policy" of reservations and missionaries in tandem dominated the decade of the 1870s, though without much success, as both Indians and Whites acknowledged. Fourth, and most important of the recommendations, was a commitment to the acculturation process "to change the savage into a civilized man."[5]

While it is true that the Doolittle Report alone did not bring about the subsequent modifications in federal policy, it certainly helped create the atmosphere for the new laws. A Congressional investigation so highly praised and widely reported carried great weight among legislators, who blindly created laws that bore little relationship to what Indians desired. The Dawes Severalty Act of 1887 represented the culmination of this nineteenth century reformism by assigning 160-acre homesteads to tribesmen who had neither the inclination nor the tools to make them prosper. For almost fifty years the Dawes Act would, in effect, undermine traditional cultures and remove over 90,000,000 acres of reservation land from Indian control. Certainly the Doolittle Report, with its inattention to Native American viewpoints and its support for the process of forced acculturation advocated by the "experts," had helped produce one of the most devastating pieces of legislation in American history.[6]

By the 1920s, even the truly conservative members of Congress and the Indian Service had come to realize that the Dawes Act had failed to accomplish its acculturation goal. Many also recognized that Indians were living in even worse conditions than when the reservations were first created. As a consequence of this new awareness, various departments of the federal government commissioned five separate studies during the decade, each of which identified failures in the Dawes Act, and all of which called for substantive changes in policy. One study focused solely on Indian irrigation projects;[7] a second emerged from the rather ineffective Board of Indian Commissioners;[8] a third resulted from a national advisory group known as the "Committee of One Hundred";[9] and the fourth represented the lengthiest publication on Indians ever issued by the federal government—a 23,000 page document based on Senate hearings and investigations.[10] But it was the fifth report which garnered the most attention and led to the formulation of government policy. Titled *The Problem of Indian Administration*, but generally referred to as the "Meriam Report" (in honor of its director), the 1928 study became the bible of reformers for the next twenty years, and probably had more direct bearing on legislation than that issued by any Indian task force in American history.[11] The survey staff comprised an assortment of historians, clergymen, organizational specialists and even one Indian, the highly acculturated Sioux, Henry Roe Cloud.

Although the Meriam Report did not offer much direct Indian testimony, it did capture the essence of Indian complaints since staff members visited a large number of reservations and truthfully recorded their findings. The 847-page document was divided into the usual topics of health, education, economic conditions, family relations, missionary activity, legal questions, structure of the Bureau of Indian Affairs, and even the new matter of urban Indians and their unique problems. But rather than merely rehashing the issues uncovered by the other studies of the period, the Meriam Report made numerous detailed recommendations. In effect, these called for a retreat from the Dawes Act, and a recognition of the value of Indian culture and communal orientation. Implicitly stated was the principle of choice between traditionalism and assimilation, and a firm conviction that Native Americans could prosper along either course if only they could take a greater share in running their own affairs.[12]

The effects of the Meriam Report were immediate for during President Herbert Hoover's administration an enlightened Bureau of Indian Affairs under Charles Rhodes and Henry Scattergood began to translate many of the suggestions into policy. Unfortunately the advent of the Great Depression shifted attention away from this reformist cause, and left the Rhodes-Scattergood administration moving in the right direction but progressing very slowly. Impetus was soon reborn with the election of President Franklin Roosevelt and his appointment of John Collier as Indian Commissioner. Under Collier's direction from 1933 to 1945, the BIA would drastically modify its approach. Most of its concepts evolved from the Meriam Report as filtered through the mind of the new commissioner. The result of this union of philosophies was the 1934 Indian Reorganization Act (Wheeler-Howard Act) whose provisions are far more extensive than this article can possibly relate.[13] Yet by focusing upon a single aspect of the Indian Reorganization Act—the one that Collier considered most critical to making the other dimensions work—we can see how the high-minded but misplaced principles of the Meriam Report could also subvert Indian needs.[14]

The central concern was the establishment of democratically elected tribal governments, which Collier felt would soon assure Indians a fair measure of self-determination. He therefore encouraged tribes to establish constitutions modeled after a BIA-drafted prototype. Furthermore, he encouraged full participation by the entire adult population of each reservation. They would elect the tribal councilmen who would then serve as the primary governing body over each separate reservation. Indians were supposed to mold the constitutions to their unique needs, and for the first time Indians would control their own daily affairs, or so claimed Collier and his colleagues.

The promise and the reality of tribal government under the Indian Reorganization Act proved quite different matters on most reservations. A majority of Indians viewed the tribal council idea with suspicion, and many refused to incorporate this aspect into the new constitutions. Collier understood the reasons for this lack of cooperation, but he was determined to implement the "democratic model" even if Indian consent was not forthcoming. His dealings with the Navajo were typical of this forced relationship. He was determined to make this, the most populous tribe on the largest reservation, into a successful test case that others would follow. Collier's bullying of the Navajo produced greater intransigence and bluntly illustrated that even under the enlightened Wheeler-Howard Act, Indian self-determination would be sacrificed to the dictates of government "experts."[15]

All across the western United States, reservations soon experienced problems with the newly imposed tribal councils. Although technically elected by the entire reservation population, tribal councilmen generally came from the ranks of the more acculturated mixed-bloods, and their pro-development attitudes clashed with the conservative views of the full-bloods. Furthermore, while enemy tribes had been forcibly settled on the same reservations during the nineteenth century, they remained suspicious of each other. Instead of cooperating with one another, they would try to totally dominate the council or else would withdraw into a shell of non-cooperation. Thus, traditional Indian patterns of factionalism were compounded and led not to Collier's grand design for a working democracy, but rather to a debilitating model of nepotism and corruption.[16] Over the next forty years tribal councils often became the main cause of, rather than the main cure for, reservation problems. Even the 1973 violent occupation of Wounded Knee, South Dakota is partially traceable to efforts by the "out-factions" to remove tribal chairman Richard Wilson from power.[17] The factionalized struggle for control continues on other reservations even today, albeit in a quieter way, and the Native American seems no closer to self-determination than when the Meriam Report and the Indian Reorganization Act first endorsed the principle.

Two Modern Problems—Misidentifying Indians and Discouraging Research

In moving away from the historical examples of the Doolittle and Meriam reports into more contemporary times, one is overwhelmed by the number of continuing problems which deserve consideration. Surprisingly, no issue is more troublesome than the government's inconsistency in defining who is an Indian, the results of which have been disastrous for Native Americans. For that reason I would like to briefly concentrate upon the definitional problem, how it came about, and why it is so important in 1982.

It is interesting that government officials and reform groups never considered definition a problem until the 1930s. They had previously believed that an accurate count was unnecessary because the "Vanishing American" was either dying off or being assimilated into the broader population. John Collier and his supporters recognized that this stereotype was no longer valid, since specific studies demonstrated that the Native American population was on the rebound. From that time on, the need to count Indians became important to bureaucrat and Indian alike. In the latter's case the issue was crucial because having one's name on tribal rolls and receiving federal recognition entitled that person to health care, educational opportunities, and a host of other human services based on treaty rights.[18]

Throughout this century, the federal definition of Indian status has rested upon three categories of population: (1) those persons of Indian ancestry who live on reservations; (2) those of at least one-quarter Indian blood, regardless of their place of residence; and (3) those peoples whose names appear on tribal rolls officially compiled during the late nineteenth and early twentieth centuries. Unfortunately, these restricted definitions omitted large numbers of people who considered themselves Indians and lived within the Indian world. No group was more harmed by this artificial distinction than were those euphemistically termed "Urban Indians." So great was their post-World War II migration to towns and cities that by 1970 well over half of the Native American population lived away from reservations. The government, despite its denials, virtually washed its hands of these people and allowed them to disappear into a twilight zone where their Indian status and attendant support programs were no longer maintained. Going to cities in search of jobs became an overwhelming liability for most since they lost the tax-exempt standing they had on reservation land, as well as crucial treaty-entitlement rights.

The proliferation of "Great Society" welfare agencies during the 1960s compounded the definitional problem as overlapping government departments used different criteria in identifying Native Americans. Only the mammoth Department of Health, Education, and Welfare demonstrated any sensitivity to the Indian viewpoint when it approved the standard that Indian organizations within a community should be empowered to define who is Indian.[19]

The example of Denver, Colorado is indicative of what happens when varying definitions are applied to public school children. In an effort to determine which schools should receive a share of Title IV federal money, as established under the Indian Education Act of 1972, Denver Public Schools and the Federal District Court applied three legalistic definitions to determine Indian enrollments. Convinced that an undercount had occurred because of the restrictive definitions, Indian leaders compiled a list of 265 additional students whom the Denver Native American community considered to be Indian. The federal district court finally agreed to the fairness of this method and allowed the 265 names to be added to the master list.[20]

On the national level, the problem inherent in defining who is Indian magnifies itself in the matter of the federal census. According to the final enumeration of 1970, slightly over 827,000 Indians were identified within the United States population.[21] Yet even before the report went to the printers, Native Americans joined other minority groups to allege that a sizable undercount had occurred. In the former's case, the issue was no longer limited to the problem of legalistic definitions, but also included the imprecise procedures utilized to count reservation dwellers. Instead of enumerating each individual family, census officials relied on sample data. While this procedure has merit in evaluating the larger national population, it is totally misleading when applied to such small population samples as are found on reservations.

The 1970 census of the Fort McDowell and Ak Chin reservations in central Arizona was based on a partial tally of the Pima and Maricopa inhabitants. Utilizing this sample and a predetermined mathematical formula, an official population figure was derived, dutifully reported to Washington, and uncritically printed in numerous government publications. An independent survey of the reservation, based on a complete rather than sample enumeration, revealed a respective sampling error of 22.4 percent and 33.8 percent within the government's figures, and yet no correction was made in the "official" statistics.[22]

A further illustration of this problem can be seen in a comparison of the federal census of 1970 with that of 1980. The later figures indicated a population of slightly over 1,418,000 Indians, or a 71.4 percent increase from a decade earlier. Obviously the Native American population did not increase *that* phenomenally within ten years. Rather the astronomically higher figures were a byproduct of better reporting methods and a concerted government effort to seek out minorities rather than simply applying mathematical formulas and samples to them.[23]

The census-taking procedures for Omaha, Nebraska were indicative of this more thorough approach. Not only was each Indian family contacted directly, but also Native American enumerators were especially hired to canvass the neighborhoods with significant Indian concentrations. More importantly, local Indian organizations were encouraged to contribute their own lists of persons who might be missed by the interview process.[24] This procedure proved worthwhile because urban Indians are generally part of a floating population which travels between reservation and city residence so often that they are likely to be overlooked in a census. Again it should be recognized that both the broad population statistics and the validation of tribal membership are crucial to the determination of treaty-entitlement funds. Likewise, tribal governments and urban Indian organizations must rely heavily on these official census figures when applying for private grants to subsidize alcoholism centers, cultural events, tutoring programs, and a host of other human services. The size of, and stipulations on, those grant funds may hinge almost entirely on the government profile of a reservation or a city population, so the counts must be more accurate than in the past.

While the census issue and the government's inconsistency in identifying Indians will continue to occupy public attention during the 1980s, an allied concern will probably receive greater coverage in Native American newspapers. This pertains to the question of access to documents which are vital to Indian land and monetary claims. Most of the post-1945 Bureau of Indian Affairs files are still maintained by the BIA, unlike the earlier records, which have long since been transferred to the National Archives and the regional Federal Records Centers. For the most part these relatively "recent" files have been stored at the Washington National Records Center in Suitland, Maryland, where they sit virtually off limits to Indians and academic researchers alike. These files do not bear a "top secret" stamp to prevent entry, but they might as well. The problem is not one of secrecy, but of access.

Persons hoping to use these materials can no longer work directly in the Suitland facility, but must wait in a crowded and dingy room of the BIA's Office of Files and Records Research in downtown Washington, D.C. The frequent delays in transporting requested files from one location to another consume precious time, as well as result in longer stays and larger hotel bills for the out-of-town researcher. Furthermore, no trained archivists preside over the BIA materials, so frequent confusion results during a search for file boxes. Clerk-typists, who double as unwilling pages, are only vaguely familiar with the records, and they do not consider these diversions to be part of their regular job. Thus a researcher's recent request for documents on the Cheyenne River and Crow Creek Sioux tribes of South Dakota resulted in the delivery of files from the Cheyenne and Crow reservations of Montana. Even though an obvious mistake had been made by BIA staff members, the researcher was still required to pay an exorbitant processing fee (a fee which, in some cases, can range up to ten dollars per hour). What would have required only a few minutes of free searching by trained archivists at the Suitland facility, had turned into a nightmare that is all too frequently repeated.[25]

Part of this change in BIA policy resulted from the Privacy Act of 1974, which correctly attempted to protect personal information from the prying eyes of unauthorized people. Unfortunately, the Bureau of Indian Affairs overutilized this well-intentioned act to discourage legitimate research. Much of this "fortress mentality" is attributable to the "we vs. they" paranoia that erupted after the 1972 Indian takeover of the BIA building and the 1973 occupation of Wounded Knee. Senior members of the Bureau are naturally hesitant to make files readily available, files that might then be utilized in lawsuits against the BIA and the Interior Department. Until the access rules are modified, trained archivists are employed, and unnecessary search fees are eliminated, Native Americans will be hampered in their claims cases, and historians will not be able to provide a complete view of post-World War II Indian policy.[26]

A Hopeful Future: The American Indian Policy Review Commission

Despite all this focus on the negative aspects of federal publications and the barriers to *bona fide* research, there are some recent developments which may modify our concept of "white man speaks with forked tongue." The most important of these developments is traceable to James Abourezk, senator from South Dakota and chairman of the Indian Affairs Subcommittee. On July 16, 1973, Abourezk introduced Senate Joint Resolution 133 for Congress to establish the American Indian Policy Review Commission (AIPRC). Its herculean task was to provide a "comprehensive review of the historical and legal developments underlying the Indians' unique relationship with the Federal Government" and to offer specific recommendations for changes in policy.[27] A year and a half later, Public Law 93-580 officially created this august body and armed it with a 2.5 million dollar budget and subpoena powers to compile the first comprehensive study of Indian affairs since the 1928 Meriam Report.

The American Indian Policy Review Commission launched a year-long investigation of nine major problem areas: (1) federal trust and treaty responsibilities, (2) tribal government, (3) structural dynamics of the BIA, (4) confusion over federal, state and tribal jurisdictions, (5) education, (6) health, (7) reservation development, (8) nonreservation Indian complaints, and (9) Indian law revision, consolidation and codification. Each investigative area was designed as a separate study, and each committee report was to be published upon completion of the entire project. More importantly, Native Americans would possess direct supervisory powers over all phases of commission activities. At the top level, five of the eleven commission positions were reserved for Indians who in no way could be tied to government jobs; the other six members came from the Senate and House of Representatives. At the second level of organization, each individual task force had to have a majority of Indian representatives. And finally, testimony for each report would come from grassroots councils to be held throughout the nation. Every effort would be made to draw urban and reservation Indians together to air complaints and make suggestions.[28] Not even the famed Meriam Report had been so promising at its inception.

Although most Native Americans, understandably, reserved judgment on the significance of the AIPRC during its 1975-1976 field hearings, tribal councils, urban Indian organizations and individuals generally cooperated with its efforts. Yet three complaints were constantly voiced during the data collection stage: (1) The hearings were being managed by Uncle Tomahawks loyal to the government's position; (2) the regional hearings were too brief to properly investigate issues beyond the

superficial level; and (3) the final reports would be filed away and forgotten before any enlightened legislation could be produced.[29] Some activist
organizations, such as the American Indian Movement, refused to cooperate on the grounds that this commission was merely another federal
attempt to legitimize further assimilationist programs and a new round
of terminationist acts like those which had created so much havoc during the 1950s and early 1960s.

Upon publication of the various AIPRC task force reports in 1976,
some of the questions seemed resolved. Indian participation in the research process had produced stinging indictments against current policy, but had also offered some common-sense recommendations for change.
The criticisms went beyond the usual rhetorical clichés and instead presented one case study after another to illustrate how the promises of
national programs often failed at the local level.[30]

Just as the Meriam Report served as the bible of the 1930s reformers,
the reports of the American Indian Policy Review Commission will be
the most frequently consulted compendiums of information for at least
the next two decades. Some of the suggestions, such as a total reorganization of the BIA structure and greater funding for Indian-run schools,
have already been partially implemented, but many of the recommendations affecting jurisdictional problems still remain in the discussion stage.
How one interprets the American Indian Policy Review Commission in
the long run of history will depend upon congressional actions during
the coming years. It certainly lays the groundwork for considerable change,
but there is no guarantee that the efforts of AIPRC members will not
fizzle in the face of congressional inattention and growing political
conservatism.

Indeed such warning signs did appear immediately after the conclusion of the AIPRC hearings. Commission Vice Chairman Lloyd Meeds
joined with fellow Congressman Jack Cunningham in sponsoring a series of bills which would further erode Indian rights. These bills included H.R. 9951, which would strip the tribes of full use of reservation
water resources and reallocate the precious commodity to white ranchers,
farmers and urban residents throughout the arid West. Furthermore,
the "Omnibus Indian Jurisdiction Act of 1977," or H.R. 9950, would
restrict the rights of tribal governments to exercise legal jurisdiction over
their own reservations. But the most threatening of the pending bills
was H.R. 9054, falsely packaged under the title "Native Americans Equal
Opportunity Act of 1977." This bill "would abrogate all treaties ever
concluded between the Indian tribes and the United States, wiping out
with one stroke the centuries-old legal basis of Indian rights."[31]

Clearly it was the intention of Meeds and Cunningham to restore the
terminationist legislation of the 1950s and to lead the powerful assault

by mineral companies, timber interests, land developers and fiscal conservatives on the protected Indian lands. Congress might have passed the bills simply because of ignorance about the effects of this legislation, but Native Americans and their allies marched across the nation in what was dubbed "The Longest Walk." With the aid of considerable press attention, they were able to explain their opposition to these bills and help educate not only congressmen but also the general public about how humanitarian-sounding legislation can be destructive of an entire people.

Although the Meeds and Cunningham bills died in committee, many Indians were left with a deeper suspicion toward the American Indian Policy Review Commission, because of Meeds' primary position within that group. Most, however, agreed with the earlier assessment of Kiowa activist lawyer Kirke Kickingbird, who had encouraged Native Americans to cooperate with the AIPRC hearings and make their voices heard. It was his observation that "for good or for ill, the resulting legislation is likely to chart the course of American Indian history into the next century."[32] To suffer in silence or withdraw behind a curtain of non-cooperation would only allow whites to formulate further policies antagonistic to Indian needs.

Kickingbird's remarks serve as the best estimation of the power of federal task force reports in the formulation of government policy. The landmark reports examined throughout this paper manifested an ambivalent nature; they were critical of existing policy, but often created new problems once their "solutions" were implemented. The "experts" who produced these documents were generally well-intentioned, but rarely did they come from a Native American background or share in the worldview of those they studied. They made decisions that seemed enlightened when applied to the broader society, but were completely in conflict with Indian cultures and desires. Perhaps the work of the American Indian Policy Review Commission and continued response from Native American groups of varying philosophies will lead us closer to the elusive goal of "Self-Determination." Only then will balladeers such as Floyd Westerman be able to write new lyrics in praise of policy reports rather than in condemnation of them.

References

1. Kate Eldridge Glaspell, "Incidents in the Life of a Pioneer," *North Dakota Historical Quarterly*, 8 (1941): 187-188.

2. U.S., Congress, Senate. *Condition of the Indian Tribes: Report of the Joint Special Committee Appointed under Joint Resolution of March 3, 1865.* Sen. Report 156, 39th Cong., 2nd sess., 1867 (serial 1279). [Doolittle Report]

3. Donald Chaput, "Generals, Indian Agents, Politicians: The Doolittle Survey of 1865, " *Western Historical Quarterly*, 3 (July 1972): 269-282.

4. Harry Kelsey, "The Doolittle Report of 1867: Its Preparation and Shortcomings," *Arizona and the West*, 17 (Summer 1975): 107-120.

5. *Condition of the Indian Tribes*, pp. 3-10.

6. The failures of the Dawes Severalty Act were outlined in a 1934 publication called for by Commissioner of Indian Affairs John Collier—U.S. Congress, House. *History of the Allotment Policy*. H.R. 7902 before House of Representatives' Committee on Indian Affairs. This has been republished in an edited and expanded form as: D.S. Otis, *The Dawes Severalty Act and the Allotment of Indian Lands*, edited by Francis Paul Prucha (Norman: University of Oklahoma Press, 1973).

7. U.S. Congress, Senate. *Review of Conditions of the Indians in the United States: Hearings Before the Committee on Indian Affairs*. S. Res. 78 and 308. 71st Cong., 2nd sess., 1930. (*The Preston-Engle Irrigation Report*, pt. 6, pp. 2210-2661.)

8. *Annual Report of the Board of Indian Commissioners to the Secretary of Interior for the Fiscal Year Ended June 30, 1926* (Washington, D.C.: Government Printing Office, 1926), pp. 3-4, 13 and 31-32.

9. *The Indian Problem*. Resolution of the Committee of One Hundred Appointed by the Secretary of the Interior and a Review of the Indian Problem, January 7, 1924 (Washington, D.C.: Government Printing Office, 1924).

10. U.S. Congress, Senate. *Survey of Conditions of the Indians in the United States: Hearings Before the Committee on Indian Affairs*. This report was an ongoing one between the 70th Congress and the 78th Congress (1928-1943), and was printed in 41 parts. It was followed by *Survey of Conditions Among the Indians of the United States. Supplemental Report*. Report No. 310, pt. 2. 78th Cong., 2nd sess., 1944.

11. *The Problem of Indian Administration* (Baltimore: Johns Hopkins Press, 1928). [Meriam Report]

12. Ibid., pp. 44 and 88.

13. S. Lyman Tyler, *A History of Indian Policy*. United States Department of the Interior, Bureau of Indian Affairs (Washington, D.C.: Government Printing Office, 1973), pp. 115-129.

14. Frederick J. Stefon, "Significance of the Meriam Report of 1928," *Indian Historian*, 7 (Summer 1975): 2-7. Contends that although the Meriam Report promoted the correct philosophy by encouraging Indian children into public schools, *implementation* of the policy under the Indian Reorganization Act and the 1934 Johnson-O'Malley Act was confused and sometimes disastrous.

15. Donald L. Parman, *The Navajos and the New Deal* (New Haven: Yale University Press, 1976), pp. 290-296.

16. Graham D. Taylor, *The New Deal and American Indian Tribalism: The Administration of the Indian Reorganization Act. 1934-1945* (Lincoln: University of Nebraska Press, 1980) pp. 39-62 and 92-118. Russel Lawrence Barsh and James Youngblood Henderson, *The Road: Indian Tribes and Political Liberty* (Berkeley: University of California Press, 1980), pp. 96-111.

17. Robert Burnette and John Koster, *The Road to Wounded Knee* (New York: Bantam Books, 1974), pp. 178-194.

18. Karl A. Funke, "Educational Assistance and Employment Preference: Who Is An Indian," *American Indian Law Review*, 4, no. 1: 1-45.

19. Stephen A. Langona, "A Statistical Profile of the Indian: The Lack of Numbers," in *Toward Economic Development for Native American Communities* (Washington, D.C.: Government Printing Office, 1969), pp. 1-6.

20. James L. Simmons, "One Little, Two Little, Three Little Indians: Counting American Indians in Urban Society," *Human Organization*, 36 (Spring 1977): 76-79.

21. U.S. Bureau of the Census. *Census of Population: 1970. Subject Reports. Final Report PC (2)-1F. American Indians* (Washington, D.C.: Government Printing Office, 1973).

22. Cary W. Meister, "The Misleading Nature of Data in the Bureau of the Census Subject Report on 1970 American Indian Population," *Indian Historian*, 11 (December 1978): 12-19.

23. *Nebraska Indian Commission Newsletter*, 6 (September 1981): 5.

24. *Nebraska Indian Territory News*, 3 (July-August 1978): 1.

25. Michael L. Lawson, "How the Bureau of Indian Affairs Discourages Historical Research," *Indian Historian*, 10 (Fall 1977): 25-27.

26. Personal letter from Michael L. Lawson (Rights Protection Branch of the Aberdeen Area Office of the BIA, Aberdeen, South Dakota), September 28, 1981. Confirms the continued existence of these problems four years after publication of his above mentioned article.

27. U.S. Congress, Senate. *Hearings on S.J. Res. 133 Before the Subcommittee on Indian Affairs of the Senate Committee on Interior and Insular Affairs*. 93rd Cong., 1st sess., 1973. p. 6.

28. Public Law 93-580, "Joint Resolution to Provide for the Establishment of the American Indian Policy Review Commission, January 2, 1975." *United States Statutes at Large*, 93rd Cong., 2nd sess., pp. 1910-1914.

29. Indian criticisms of the initial stages of the American Indian Policy Review Commission were articulated in the following issues of the national Indian newspaper *Wassaja*: January-February 1975, p. 19; June 1975, p. 2; September 1976, p. 2; November-December 1976, p. 2.

30. For an assessment of each of the individual volumes issued in 1976 by the American Indian Policy Review Commission, *see* Michael L. Tate, "Red Power: Government Publications and the Rising Indian Activism of the 1970s," *Government Publications Review*, 8, no. 6, (1981): 499-518.

31. Quoted in "Bills Threaten Indian Rights," *Indian Natural Resources*, (December 1977), p. 7. Bruce Johansen and Roberto Maestas, *Wasi' chu: The Continuing Indian Wars* (New York: Monthly Review Press, 1979), pp. 208-214.

32. Kirke Kickingbird, "The American Indian Policy Review Commission: A Prospect for Future Change in Federal Indian Policy," *American Indian Law Review*, 3, no. 2 (1975): 243-253.

TESTING THE QUALITY OF REFERENCE SERVICE PROVIDED BY ACADEMIC DEPOSITORY LIBRARIES: A PILOT STUDY

By Peter Hernon and Charles R. McClure

General reference services in academic, public, and special libraries have been investigated by hidden or unobtrusive testing and by the collection of empirical data relating to the quality of responses given to questions asked by people posing as clientele of that library. Published and unpublished reports examining the quality of reference services provided by staff members responsible for depository collections, however, appear to be nonexistent. Due to the vast amount of government publications distributed through the depository program each year as well as the cost of the depository program to both the government and individual libraries, an assessment of the quality of reference services provided with resources readily available to depository libraries appears to be needed.

The documents community does not know the probability of success when library clientele request information that clearly can be obtained from government publications or through the referral process. Furthermore, factors that impact on the likelihood of obtaining accurate answers to government publication reference questions are currently unknown. Knowledge of the quality of reference services and of the factors affecting this quality can assist government document librarians in developing strategies to improve existing services. The baseline data gathered should also provide insights into the effectiveness of the depository program operated by the Government Printing Office (GPO). At the same time, study findings can be compared to those taken from the general reference field and can be used to identify similarities and dissimilarities between general reference and document reference services.

The purpose of this chapter is to present the results of a study that assessed the quality of reference service provided at a sampling of academic government document depository libraries. After discussing the literature related to the general topic, the research design of the study will be discussed; results will be presented; and some implications from the data will be raised. Overall, the study suggests that the quality of academic depository reference service, as measured in this study, is quite low. Furthermore, the study demonstrates that, on an average, a person attempting to obtain factual and bibliographic information from the depository libraries investigated has approximately a thirty-seven percent probability of obtaining a correct answer.

Literature Review

The unobtrusive testing of reference service can be traced back to a dissertation by Terence Crowley in the late 1960s and a later dissertation by Thomas Childers. Both studies were published in one volume in 1971.[1] These studies focused on public libraries in New Jersey and involved testing by both telephone and in-person queries. They showed substantial differences between the claims made by reference librarians and the results gathered from such testing. Librarians were much less effective in answering factual reference questions (e.g., those relating to changing political figures and current affairs) than was previously thought. In fact, they could only answer approximately half of the questions correctly and seemed to be unaware that they were disseminating obsolete or incorrect information in answer to the others. Although the studies contained some government-related questions (e.g., "Would you give me the name of the Secretary of Commerce?" and "How did Senator Case vote on the 1957 Civil Rights Bill?"), testing was limited to general reference staff.

In a study of the quality of service provided to factual questions, Marcia Jean Myers discovered that even when academic libraries owned an appropriate information source, staff members might not consult it or know how to use it. They might even misinterpret the information contained therein. Furthermore, staff members infrequently volunteered the sources of their responses.[2]

Thomas Childers conducted unobtrusive testing of fifty-seven libraries of the Suffolk Cooperative Library System. As with the other studies, he included some questions pertaining to governments and their publishing programs (e.g., "Where can I get a federal publication called *Final Report: President's Task Force on Communication Policy*, published in 1967?"). In addition to studying the accuracy of the responses, this investigation was the first to find out "about the library staff's readiness to 'negotiate' a question."[3] The libraries, in several instances, "were scored not on the correctness of the answer they gave, but on their success in arriving at the ultimate step [the actual reference question]."[4] Childers also followed up on the referral process and "tested the response by any resource agency mentioned by a library."[5]

The studies discussed in this section show that unobtrusive testing can be applied to reference librarianship and that such research provides insights into the quality of service extended to questions requiring factual and bibliographic information. Based on this research, it was proved that unobtrusive testing could be used in the documents field as a valid means of assessing the quality of depository reference service.

Research Questions

Since previous research has not examined the quality of reference services provided by documents staff members, this study should be regarded as exploratory. The research questions can be stated thus:

- Will the quality of government publication reference services differ significantly according to highest degree offered (baccalaureate, master's-granting, and doctoral) at the institution of which the library is a part?
- Will the quality of government publication reference services differ significantly according to the percentage of item numbers selected by depositories, the number of library volumes, the total library budget, the total number of library professional staff, or the number of government document FTE professionals or paraprofessionals?

The investigation of these research questions was limited to reference services provided in academic depository libraries.

Methodology

Population and Sampling Frame

The academic depository libraries eligible for investigation were from the Northeast and Southwest United States, the regions in which the investigators reside. By selecting institutions within these two regions, the expenses involved in data collection could be minimized and the time frame for gathering the data reduced.

Academic depository libraries from these two regions were stratified by the highest degree offering of the institution. Institutional control (public or private) was not a major factor in stratification, due to the distribution of the institutions within the two regions. Random sampling from each stratum (baccalaureate, master's-granting, and doctoral) produced the seventeen institutions at which the unobtrusive testing would occur. The actual study sites will not be identified, and data analysis will protect their anonymity. However, it can be disclosed that five of the institutions selected were baccalaureate, four were master's-granting, and eight were doctoral institutions.

Test Questions

Quality of government document reference services was equated with the number of correct answers given to a predetermined list of reference questions which could be answered primarily by the use of government publication information sources. The test questions were developed according to the following criteria:

- The questions are reflective of the types asked by the public in search of government information.
- The questions are answerable, to a large degree, from more than one source.
- The questions are answerable with factual information or bibliographic references.
- The questions reflect a wide range of document types and time frames.
- The questions are answerable from individual depository collections or are dependent on the referral process.[6]
- The questions are answerable from resources dealing with the U.S. government. These resources should be at the disposal of depository libraries.

Based on these criteria, questions were culled from the collection of the GPO bookstore in Boston, Massachusetts, as well as from among those received by the City of Boston Consumer Council, the U.S. Bureau of the Census Regional Office, Boston, and from documents librarians known to the researchers but not affiliated with any of the seventeen institutions selected for investigation. In addition, the preliminary list included some questions of interest to the researchers and some from studies testing the quality of general reference service.

The initial pool of test questions and their answers were submitted to documents librarians at four academic depositories (two from each area) of the study population but outside the seventeen institutions where the investigation was to take place. During the months of August and September, 1981, these librarians criticized the test questions and suggested rewordings as well as questions to add or delete. On the basis of their comments, the list was revised and finalized. It was decided that half of the study questions would be administered over the telephone and that the other half would be presented in person, with proxies posing as clientele of that institution or as members of the general public trying to satisfy a particular information need.

Administration of Test Questions

From October through December, 1981, proxies administered the test questions at the seventeen libraries. These proxies consisted of students enrolled during the fall term in the documents courses at Simmons College and the University of Oklahoma.[7] In order to ensure the collection of valid data, the investigators discussed the project with interested students, conducted training sessions, coordinated and monitored the data collection process, and encouraged students to maintain an interest in the project after the completion of the school term. Once the questions had been administered and the responses obtained, the proxies completed the "Reference Question Tabulation Sheet," which is reprinted in the Appendix (Figure 7-1). The investigators discussed the answers with the students to ensure accuracy, consistency, and completeness in data collection. The investigators also double-checked all responses to ensure consistency in the reporting of responses.

When administering the questions and tabulating the results, student proxies were reminded to follow these guidelines as much as possible:

- Ask the question sincerely and accurately. Appear to be conducting research or writing a paper for which the information is necessary.
- Do not have the "Reference Question Tabulation Sheet" or the list of questions out in the open during administration. Remember the question, and complete the tabulation sheet after the administration.
- Attempt to ask the questions during times of the day in which one could expect to find a professional librarian in the documents area or in the library.

Many documents departments are understaffed and lack professional staff members to cover the documents reference desk during all the hours the library is open. However, for certain student proxies, evenings and weekends might be more convenient for administration of the in-person test questions. Students were encouraged to vary the hours of their visits, but were instructed to approach whomever staffed the documents public service desk. If that person accepted the question, testing proceeded. In those cases in which students were encouraged to return when a documents librarian was on duty, the question was administered at a later time. Even though the testing process may have involved other than the professional staff members, it indicates the type of service that library clientele can expect in their search for government information. Adverse findings and poor service might suggest the need for more in-service training programs and referral to staff members with a master's degree in library science, a subject equivalency, or knowledge about gaining access to government publications/information.

Students were reminded that unobtrusive testing requires the collection of data from participants without their knowing about the real purpose of the question. Students were asked not to discuss the project or to reveal the study sites while the research was in progress. If participating libraries and their staffs realized that they were being studied, their behavior (and thus, the findings) would be affected. Students also were asked not to discuss the project with students in other classes or with friends, since the information could conceivably get back to the participating libraries and invalidate the findings. Furthermore, students agreed not to disseminate information about an individual library's scores. All the data collected were to be confidential and under no circumstances would be linked to an individual library.

Unobtrusive Testing

As discovered during the pre-test phase, some documents librarians feel uncomfortable with unobtrusive testing. They questioned the purpose for which such data would be used, and raised ethical considerations about testing people unaware of the real nature of the inquiry. It should be remembered, however, that such testing has been used in the general reference field as well as outside librarianship for a number of years.[8] Unobtrusive testing is a legitimate means for data collection; it provides insights that cannot easily be obtained otherwise.

Documents librarians may feel uncomfortable with two other aspects of this study. First, the selection of the test questions, and second, the fact that some paraprofessional staff members may have been tested. It is our belief that we have taken steps to minimize the validity of such criticisms. The test questions, which were developed according to specific criteria, were subjected to a rigorous pre-test and gained the approval of professional depository librarians. Some of the questions selected for the study had actually been asked at the pre-test sites. Staff members at these libraries went through their lists of the reference questions to be asked and shared with the investigators others they believed appropriate for this study. The investigators feel that the quality of reference service can be evaluated any time a library provides such service. Still, the investigators want to point out that this is an exploratory study, one we hope will lead to further analyses of depository reference services.

Findings

The following analysis is based on: (1) the responses to the twenty questions asked at each depository; (2) data collected relating to the provision of referral service, first contact answer,* duration of reference interview, and other variables suggested by the "Reference Question Tabulation Sheet," and (3) institutional data such as library budget, the number of volumes held, the number of staff, and the percent of item numbers selected. The completed "Reference Question Tabulation Sheets" were coded and entered into a computer for analysis via SPSS, a statistical software analysis program.

Because of the richness of the data, numerous analysis techniques can be performed among the three general categories of data outlined above. Further, since the data come from a sample of ten depositories in the Northeastern United States and seven depositories in the Southwestern United States, regional analysis of the data is possible. Nonetheless, it should be stressed that the sample size of seventeen academic depository libraries—which resulted in a total of 340 questions for analysis— although limited, has great analytic potential. Thus, the following findings are only a partial, preliminary presentation of areas seen by the investigators as being of special interest to readers of these proceedings. Final data analysis and presentation of complete findings from this study will be published in a forthcoming monograph.[9]

Of primary importance is the accuracy with which the twenty questions were answered, that is, the percentage of correct answers provided by the depositories. Table 7-1 provides a summary of correct answers for each question for both the Northeastern and Southwestern regions. On an average, Northeastern depository libraries answered 49% of the questions correctly and Southwestern libraries answered 20% correctly; the overall average of all questions answered correctly was 37%. The table

---

*The first contacted staff member either gave a definite answer to the reference question, or told the student proxy to come to the library for assistance or to come back when a documents librarian was on duty.

Table 7-1: Summary of Correct Answers by Region

Question Number	Percent Answered Correctly, NE (N=10)	Percent Answered Correctly, SW (N=7)	Percent Answered Correctly, ALL
1	30	14	24
2	10	0	6
3	40	0	24
*4	50	14	35
*5	40	29	35
6	30	14	24
*7	100	43	77
8	40	14	29
*9	40	57	47
10	10	14	12
11	60	29	47
*12	50	14	35
*13	70	29	53
14	80	0	47
*15	70	29	53
*16	80	86	82
17	50	0	29
18	10	14	12
*19	50	0	29
*20	70	14	47
	49% Average	20% Average	37% Average

*indicates question delivery by telephone

also suggests a wide variance of correct answers, depending upon the nature of the individual questions. For example, all of the Northeastern depositories answered question 7 (asking for information about a legislative history) correctly, but only 10% answered question 18 (inquiring about a government map) correctly. Further, the table suggests that, regardless of the region, questions asked over the telephone rather than in person were more likely to be answered correctly. Finally, the significant difference between percentage of correct answers to similar questions in the Northeast versus the Southwest deserves additional investigation.

The relationship between correct answers and the percentage of depository items selected by the library is presented in Table 7-2. Apparently the amount of items selected does not significantly affect the percentage of correct answers. For Northeastern depository libraries, 50% of the depositories that selected less than 50% of the items provided correct answers, while 45% of the depositories with more than 50% of

Table 7-2: Summary of Correct Answers by Percent of Items Selected

	Depositories Selecting 50% or Less of Items		Depositories Selecting 51% or More of Items	
	NE (n=8)	SW (n=4)	NE (n=2)	SW (n=3)
Correct Answer (in percent)	50	20	45	21
Partial Answer (in percent)	8	11	18	13
Incorrect Answer (in percent)	42	69	37	66
	100%	100%	100%	100%

the items selected provided correct answers. A similar breakdown for Southwestern depositories can also be seen. In short, the percentage of items selected by a depository does not impact on the percentage of correct answers provided by government documents staff members.

Of some interest are the surprising findings presented in Table 7-3, which examines the percentage of correct answers by delivery method (telephone or in-person). For example, for Southwestern depositories, 29% of all answers given by telephone were correct as compared to only 10% in-person. For Northeastern depositories, 64% of all telephone responses were correct as compared to only 35% of the in-person responses. Clearly, the data from this table suggest that the probability of obtaining a correct answer is at least twice as great by asking the question over the telephone rather than in person. The explanation of this finding will require additional investigation.

Data were also collected regarding whether depository staff members provided referral service and the percentage of questions which received a "first contact answer." A "first contact answer," to repeat, is defined as any response, regardless of whether it was correct or incorrect, providing a specific answer to the reference question. Table 7-4 provides one illustration of referrals given when the librarian was unable to supply an answer. For example, on question number 1 (attempting to locate a nineteenth century document), 29% of the responses did not involve any answer, except perhaps that the answer could not be found at that depository or that the staff member simply did not know. However, for that same question, in only 22% of those instances in which an answer was not given was there *also* referral to another information provider or person as a means of answering the question. Taking the averages for all the questions suggests that 28% of the responses from library staff members could not be classified as answers (either correct or incorrect). For

Table 7-3: Summary of Correct Answers by Delivery Method

	By Telephone Question Delivery*		In-Person Question Delivery*	
	NE	SW	NE	SW
Correct Answer (in percent)	64	29	35	10
Partial Answer (in percent)	8	10	13	14
Incorrect Answer (in percent)	28	61	52	76
	100%	100%	100%	100%

*A chi-square test of significance indicates that the relationship between the method of delivery and correct answer (for both the Northeast and Southwest) is significant at the .01 level

all those cases in which answers were not supplied, only an average of 17% were then referred to another information provider. Once again, there is a wide range of variance on the questions when analyzed individually, which suggests that specific attributes of the questions may affect the likelihood of it being referred. For example, question 10 (seeking the citation of a publication of the Federal Aviation Administration) had an unusually high percentage of referral, due in part to the fact that the question is related to this particular agency. Since there is a regional FAA training center in Oklahoma City, depositories in the Southwest referred the proxies to that center. However, there was limited referral for all the remaining questions. Of the mere 53 referrals offered, 28% were to regional depositories and 28% were to another librarian in the same library. Although additional analysis is necessary regarding the referral of questions, it appears that limited referral was provided and that in many instances, when the proxy was told that an answer could not be provided (for whatever reason), no attempt was made to refer him/her to some other information provider.

In response to the research questions posed earlier in this chapter, the preliminary analysis of data suggests that the number of correct responses cannot be explained by the highest degree offered at that institution. Further, no significant relationships appear to exist between the number of correct responses and other institutional variables such as the number of staff members, library budget, the percentage of items selected, or the number of volumes held. However, the delivery method (telephone

Table 7-4: Summary of Referral Given with No Answer on First Contact

Question Number	Percent of No Answers on First Contact	Percent Referred to Another Information Provider
1	29	22
2	35	40
3	29	12
*4	24	17
*5	24	36
6	29	30
*7	24	6
8	29	0
*9	18	12
10	29	59
11	24	0
*12	29	6
*13	35	12
14	18	6
*15	29	12
*16	12	0
17	29	12
18	29	17
*19	41	35
*20	41	6
	28% Average	17% Average

* indicates question delivery by telephone

versus in-person) is significantly related to the quality of reference services provided at the academic depository libraries examined.

The above findings represent only a sampling of the data analysis that will be undertaken in the forthcoming monograph. For example, there will be additional analyses that correlate the number of correct answers to institutional variables; that look at the referral process; that provide a question-by-question examination of factors that contributed to answers being given; and that examine other question-related variables such as the duration of the reference interview and library budget. Nonetheless, the preliminary data presented in this chapter outline the general nature of the findings.

Only 37% of the 340 questions administered were answered correctly. The percentage of correct answers does not appear to be affected by the percentage of depository items selected by the individual depositories; those with less than 50% item selection have approximately the same percentage of correct answers as those with greater than 50% item selection. The likelihood of obtaining a correct answer is increased by at least twice if the question is asked over the telephone rather than in-person. Respondents receiving no answer to their question receive limited referral to other information providers. And the percentage of correct answers by academic depositories in the Northeast is more than twice that of academic depositories in the Southwest.

Conclusion

The findings of this exploratory study conjure up issues and questions relating to library management and the administration of the depository library program. First, public access to government publications encompasses more than bibliographic control of the documents and their physical availability in libraries. It also requires knowledgeable reference service about what is contained in depository collections and about how to gain access to additional source material, whether in published or unpublished form.

For those of us who are library users, the findings of this study might encourage us to pose questions requiring factual data by telephone rather than visiting depository collections in person. If library staff members refuse to take the question over the telephone, we could then visit the library; however, visiting the library may result in less distinguished assistance. Perhaps documents staff members are willing to spend more search-time in reply to telephone inquiries than to in-person ones. After all, they can proceed in a more leisurely way, since they have the option of calling the person back.

The study seems to call into question the validity of gathering and reporting reference statistics that merely identify the number of reference questions answered by the documents staff on a daily, weekly, monthly, and annual basis. It would be more meaningful to determine how well information needs are being met and to revise the *Guidelines for the Depository Library System* (as adopted by the Depository Library Council, October 1977) so that it can take into account program goals and objectives as well as measures of performance.

It would seem that 37 percent is a low overall average for correct responses, especially since the documents staff members tested infrequently provide referral service. Library users can obviously experience great variation in the quality of reference service depending on the nature of the individual question asked. These findings suggest that depository libraries ought to decide

- what types of reference questions they should attempt to address. (Should they attempt to answer any question involving a request for government information?)

- whether they can provide the same level of service for all questions asked.
- whether they are responsible for the accuracy and currency of the information they disseminate.

The GPO itself should be concerned about the answers to these questions as well as to such questions as:

- What are the implications for the depository library program as an interlocking network when users experience divergent levels of service and are not referred to depositories better equipped to handle certain requests?
- What is an acceptable level of correct responses, and should depository libraries be responsible for the answers provided to clientele?
- Should documents staff members be required to participate in continuing education programs and to receive advanced training?
- Is the depository library program cost/beneficial? (If it is not, should the GPO make a financial commitment for the improvement of reference services?)
- Can a national program to promote the collections and services of depository libraries be regarded as successful, if citizens encounter undistinguished reference service?

In conclusion, the quality of documents reference service has implications beyond the immediate institution. It is reflective of the depository library program, its goals and objectives. Furthermore, it raises questions about the appropriateness of maintaining a system unable to provide better than 37 percent accuracy to reference questions calling for depository resources. We all have an interest in ascertaining the quality of reference service provided by depository libraries and in wanting to see improvements made wherever they might be needed.

Limitations

Based on the nature of the research design, the investigators realize that the data can be applied only to academic depository institutions within the two regions. Other depository libraries with similar institutional characteristics to those reported in this study, however, may be able to draw useful comparisons and implications pertinent to improving the quality of their documents reference services. It should be noted that depository collections housed at law school libraries were not investigated.[10]
    The data apply only to reference service for questions of a factual and bibliographic nature, covering the U.S. government and its publication/information program. Another limitation is the assumption that the aca-

demic depositories investigated maintained a "basic reference collection" of document-related publications such as the *CIS Index* and the *American Statistics Index*. In some cases, these or other "basic" document reference sources were not available for the particular depository under investigation.

Recommendations for Further Study

A number of topics emerged during the process of completing the study which merit additional investigation. These include:

- Comparison of service between general reference and documents collections. It might be questioned whether the general or central reference area, in depository libraries with separate government documents collections, provides less effective reference service on document-related questions than would the government documents department. Criteria for effectiveness would focus on the accuracy and speed of the response, and willingness to engage in referral, if necessary. Such studies might use our same test questions but delete references to the fact that government publications are sought.
- Examination of other types of depositories (e.g., public library and law school depositories) and comparisons of depository types.
- Examination of the referral process; in those cases where documents staff members suggest referral, an effort could be made to determine the accuracy of the response given by the referral source.
- Examination of service provided solely by professional staff.
- Comparison of service provided by professional and nonprofessional staff.
- Examination of test questions reflecting the publishing programs of other levels of government.
- Determination of the ability of documents staff members to negotiate reference questions. Given a general question, will they attempt to identify specific information needs?
- Assessment of the basic documents reference tools available within the depository library and their physical location related to the general reference desk or the documents department.

References

1. Terence Crowley and Thomas Childers, *Information Service in Public Libraries: Two Studies* (Metuchen, N.J.: Scarecrow, 1971).
2. Marcia Jean Myers, "The Effectiveness of Telephone Reference/Information Services in Academic Libraries in the Southeast," Ph.D dissertation, Florida State University, 1979. For a discussion of the literature on testing the quality of

reference service, *see* the literature review section contained in Myers' dissertation. *See also* Jassim Muhammad Jirjees, "The Accuracy of Selected Northeastern College Library Reference/Information Telephone Services in Responding to Factual Inquiries," Ph.D. dissertation, Rutgers University, 1981.

3. Thomas Childers, "The Test of Reference," *Library Journal*, 105 (April 15, 1980): 925.

4. Ibid., p. 926.

5. Ibid.

6. Information and referral may be defined as "facilitating the link between a person with a need and the service, activity, information, or advice outside the library which can meet the need." Thomas Childers, "Trends in Public Library I & R Services," *Library Journal*, 104 (October 1, 1979): 2036.

7. We wish to acknowledge our gratitude to the students who collected the data. The students participating from Simmons College were Karyn Franzek, David Gordon, Christine Mandel, Laurence Prusak, Margot Rendall, and M. Pauline LeBlanc Wood. Those participating from the University of Oklahoma include Terresa Knott, Michele Moore Lovelace, Melinda Shirley Sattler, Deborah Anna Bareff, Laurence O. Keys, Kathryn Joachim Meuaquaya, Michele S. King, Lisa M. Landrum, Joan Schipper, Vicky Baker, Mona L. Lemmings, and Elba F. Brooks.

8. *See* Eugene J. Webb et al., *Unobtrusive Measures* (Chicago: Rand McNally, 1966).

9. Charles R. McClure and Peter Hernon, *Improving the Quality of Reference Service for Government Publications* (Chicago: American Library Association, forthcoming). This book reprints all the test questions.

10. Readers interested in law school depositories should *see* Ann Armstrong and Judith C. Russell, "Public Access," *Information World*, 1 (October 1979): 1 and 11.

APPENDIX

Figure 7-1. Reference Question Tabulation Sheet

Library Name _____   Dates Administered _____   Person/s Administering Questions _____

Total Library Volumes _____   Total Budget _____   Government Doc FTE Professionals _____

Total Library Professional Staff _____   Percent of Items Selected _____   Government Doc FTE Paraprofessionals _____

Reference Question	Time Ques-tion Ask-ed	Total Time of Reference Interview	Phone Or In Person	Cor-rect Answer	Par-tial Answer	Wrong Data	Don't Know	Don't Have Sources Needed	Other (Describe)	To Another Librarian in-side Same Lib	To Gov't Agency	To GPO Bookstore	Reg Dep	To Another Docs Lib Outside Lib	Patron Asked Return At Later Date For Answer	Other (Describe)
						If Incorrect or No Answer							*Referral*			
													"Come back when Docs Lib on duty" Census Bureau or State Data Center			

COMMENTS OR ADDITIONAL EXPLANATION:

THE NATURE OF RESEARCH IN GOVERNMENT PUBLICATIONS: PRELIMINARY FINDINGS*

By John V. Richardson, Jr.

Introduction

Problem

Since 1928 when the University of Illinois accepted Jerome K. Wilcox's thesis, approximately 260 specialization papers, theses, and doctoral dissertations have been accepted by North American library schools. Even though these works constitute a major source of knowledge about the field, few investigators have studied these contributions. Consequently, we have almost no information about who has written about what and how things have changed over time. As a consequence of the present study, students can see where their work fits into the total research picture. Second, advisers can better understand the importance of their role and be better prepared to counsel their students. Third, practitioners wishing to hire students will know more about particular schools and advisers. Other practitioners can learn what the state-of-the-art is, and where they may want to do more reading.

---

*Oryx Press will publish an in-depth analysis of this topic as a monograph tentatively entitled, *Graduate Research in Government Publications*, some time late in 1983 or early 1984.

© 1983 John V. Richardson, Jr.

Assumptions

There are two. First, that specialization papers, theses, and doctoral dissertations are a significant enough segment of our professional knowledge-base to warrant separate analysis. And second, that these studies reflect significant topics in need of study; in other words, they are not simply academic exercises (although it is agreed that "the thesis is the best known method of training the candidate in the methods of research").[1]

Objectives

The three objectives of this study were:

1. To define the following basic characteristics of graduate research:
- Who (the institution, the adviser, and the advisee).
- What [type of study, level of government, functional activity (process), context (type of library), content (research methodology), and total pagination].
- When (date of completion).
2. To further explore selected variables and establish relationships.
3. To postulate and test several hypotheses.

Methodology

Population

Steps were taken to ensure that a complete list of theses on government publications was obtained. The first step was a comprehensive search through the appropriate general indexes:

1. *Library Literature*, 1921 to present. "Library Schools—Theses" and "Library Schools—Specialization Papers."
2. Alan Schorr, *Government Documents in the Library Literature, 1909-1974* (Ann Arbor, Michigan: Pierian Press, 1976).
3. Shirley Magnotti, *Master's Theses in Library Science, 1960-1974* (Troy, NY: Whitston Publishing Company, 1975 and 1976).
4. Gail A. Schlachter and Dennis Thomison, *Library Science Dissertations* (Littleton, CO: Libraries Unlimited, 1974).
5. *Government Publications Review*'s "Thesis in Documents," 1976 to present.
6. *Master's Abstracts*, 1962-   , v. 19, no. 1 (1980/81).

7. *Library and Information Science Abstracts*, vol. 1 (1969) to present.
8. P. J. Taylor, *Library and Information Studies in the United Kingdom.*

This was followed by extensive correspondence with library school faculty and deans. Together, these two steps yielded a total of 260 theses.

Content Analysis and Coding

The bibliographic citations and abstracts for the theses were examined and coded for machine-readable format. Following keypunching, the data were analyzed using the *Statistical Package for the Social Sciences* (SPSS).

Findings: General Characteristics

Type of Study

As shown in Figure 8-1, more MLS theses (141; 54 percent) have been completed than specialization papers or reports (90; 35 percent), and more papers than doctoral dissertations (22; 9 percent). While it is difficult to estimate the total number of theses and specialization papers accepted by ALA-accredited schools, that is not the case with dissertations. Between 1930 and 1980, 915 dissertations were accepted; consequently, the 22 doctoral dissertations on government publications constitute only 2.4 percent of the total.

Level of Government

What emerges most clearly from the data is that the graduate work deals with five discrete levels of government. Practically speaking, there has been no multilevel (i.e., comparative) study. Of the meager number of studies, two of the five examined municipal, state and federal governments; another two, federal and foreign governments; only one student focused on state and local governments. Not surprisingly, two-thirds of all studies examined the federal level. Others concerned themselves with state, followed by foreign, U.N., and municipal governments.

This finding suggests that the federal level is the primary object of research; but is it because this level is most worthy of study, or where most of the jobs are? Perhaps it is further evidence of the pervasive influence that the federal government has on our lives. Understandably, in a documents course the student encounters the federal level first. Apparently he then finds significant problems to study only at that level. Should this be so?

Figure 8-1: Preliminary Findings

I. **General Characteristics**

A. Type (N=260)

MLS Thesis	141; 54%
MLS Paper	90; 35%
Dissertation	22; 9%

B. Level of Government (N=260)

Federal	169; 66%
State	44; 17%
Foreign	27; 10%
U.N.	10; 4%
Municipal	5; 2%
Comparative	5; 2%

C. Functional Activity (N=131)

Administration	30; 23%
Cataloging	23; 18%
Use	22; 17%
Indexing	21; 16%
Sel. & Acq.	16; 12%
Classification	6; 5%
Cat. & Class.	6; 5%
Reference	4; 3%
Circulation	3; 2%

D. Context

Special	23; 30%
University	16; 21%
Public	11; 15%
School	11; 15%
College	7; 10%

E. Research Method (N=247)

High quantitative	10; 4%
Low quantitative	42; 17%
Analytical	45; 18%
Descriptive	37; 15%
Historical	28; 11%
How-to-do-it	7; 3%
Practice	78; 32%

F. Pagination (N=249)

Range	14-560 pp.
Mode	49
Median	80
Mean	114

G. Date

1928-37:	16
1938-47:	34
1948-57:	61
1958-67:	61
1968-77:	65

Functional Activity

More than half of the studies focused on a particular activity related to government publications. Indeed, the field of government documents is a microcosm of the entire library profession. The processes studied most often (listed in declining order of frequency) are: administration, cataloging, use, indexing, and selection and acquisition.

Institutional Context

More often than not, the graduate research was conducted without a particular type of library in mind, but in 30 percent of the studies, authors examined government publications in the context of a particular library or information center.

If the two categories "university" and "college" are subsumed under one heading, "academic," then they tie for the most frequently studied institutional context. I suspect this is the case because most depositories (the federal ones, at least) are within academic institutions. The fact that special library contexts ranked as highly as they did is due to the correspondingly special problems documents in such situations present for study.

Pagination

As a minor part of this study, data were collected on the total number of pages. Data were available for two-thirds of the graduate literature. Students' papers ranged from 14 to 560 pages; the mean was 114, the median 80, and the mode 49. The median test revealed, not surprisingly, that doctoral dissertations were significantly longer than other types of studies.

Date of Completion

Since 1928 almost five theses have been completed each year. Five years stand out as peak production periods: 1977 (13), 1956 (12), 1950 (9), 1955 (9), and 1966 (9). However, the basic patterns show research output doubling for the first thirty years: 1928-1937 (16), 1938-1947 (34), 1948-1957 (61), 1958-1967 (61), and 1968-1977 (65). In the last five years, 1977-1982, twenty-three were completed. We seem to have reached a plateau and possibly begun a decline in the latest ten year period, 1977-1987. Overall, however, the distribution is an almost classic bell-shaped curve, with the mean and median year at 1960. Assuming library schools continue to require some type of thesis, the general level of output does not appear likely to change in the near future.

Institution

Table 8-1 shows the overall research output by institution. Clearly, there are at least two major centers in the United States for the study of government publications. The fact that the University of Illinois is at the top of the list today appears to be an historical artifact (due to its long-standing thesis requirement and several influential faculty advisers), since the school has not accepted a thesis on government publications since 1966. The University of North Carolina, on the other hand, *first* accepted a thesis in 1956. It has moved into second place, continues to be a

Table 8-1: Centers for Graduate Research in Government Publications

Position Number	Institutional Affiliation	Number of Students N = 260	Relative Percentage	Cumulative Percentage
1	University of Illinois	36	13.8%	13.8%
2	University of North Carolina	33	12.7	26.5
3	Catholic University	21	8.1	34.6
4	University of Chicago	14	5.4	40.0
4	University of Denver	14	5.4	45.4
6	Case Western Reserve	13	5.0	50.4
7	Long Island University	12	4.6	55.0
7	University of Michigan	12	4.6	59.6
9	Columbia University	10	3.8	63.4
9	University of Washington	10	3.8	67.2
11	University of California, LA	8	3.1	70.3
11	Kent State University	8	3.1	73.4
13-39	27 Other Universities	69	26.5	99.9

Source: Richardson, "The Nature of Research in Government Publications," UCLA 1982.

significant contributor in terms of percentage, and will shortly overtake the University of Illinois.

Interestingly, the top twelve institutions account for 73 percent of the graduate studies completed. The top three alone account for more than a third, while the top six fully account for half.

The ranking of several institutions is due to the influence of one individual, whereas elsewhere several faculty members have influenced the relative ranking. At the University of Washington and the University of California, Los Angeles, Dorothy Bevis and John V. Richardson, Jr. respectively have helped place their institution in the top ten. At the University of Denver, on the other hand, many faculty members have supervised theses on documents (e.g., Alfred J. Coco, Oliver Field, James Foyle, and Rowena Swanson). The same can be said for the University of Chicago (Carleton Joeckel, T.H. Tsien, and Howard Winger).

At the doctoral level there are still only a handful of schools producing dissertations on documents. The top five schools are: the University of Chicago (4), Columbia University (4), Indiana University (3), the University of Michigan (3), the University of Illinois (2), and the University of Pittsburgh (2). Rutgers University, Texas Women's University, the University of Southern California, and the University of Toronto have each accepted one dissertation.

Adviser

Table 8-2 reveals the most influential advisers, as defined by total thesis output. The position of the University of Illinois as the leading school was due to four individuals, now deceased: Rose B. Phelps, Ethel Bond, Phineas L. Windsor, and Anne M. Boyd. Each was well-known in his or her own right for making contributions to documents librarianship. Whether the University of Illinois will hold the top position much longer appears to be highly unlikely, although it should be noted that Terry Weech and Kathleen Heim have joined the faculty there. The University of North Carolina should overtake the University of Illinois shortly because Ridley R. Kessler continues to supervise students there.

As a group, the top fourteen advisers have supervised 33 percent of all theses. More narrowly stated, the top ten have supervised 27 percent, and the top five have supervised 13 percent.

Additional Research

This study is being extended to include several fronts. The following list is only suggestive:

Table 8-2: Influential Faculty Advisers in Government Publications

Position Number	Individual Adviser	Institutional Affiliation	Number of Advisees	Quantitative Low or High	Analytico-Descriptive	Historical Research	Practice Work
1	Helen M. Focke	C.W.R.U.	10	1	3	1	5
2	Ridley R. Kessler	U,N.C.	8	2	2	1	3
2	James J. Kortendick	Catholic	8	1	1	6	-
2	Rose B. Phelps	Illinois	8	-	2	-	6
5	Ethel Bond	Illinois	7	-	2	-	5
5	Phineas L. Windsor	Illinois	7	-	2	-	5
5	Dorothy Bevis	Washington	7	-	-	-	7
8	Anne M. Boyd	Illinois	5	-	3	-	2
8	Edith M. Coulter	U.C.B.	5	1	2	-	2
8	John V. Richardson	U.C.L.A.	5	2	2	1	-
11	John M. Goudeau	Florida State	4	-	-	-	4
11	Doralyn J. Hickey	U.N.C.	4	1	2	-	1
11	Frederic J. O'Hara	Long Island	4	1	1	-	2
11	Agnes L. Reagen	Emory	4	4	-	-	-

SOURCE: Richardson, "The Nature of Research in Government Publications," UCLA 1982.

1) What is the role of gender in choosing government publications topics?
2) Are these studies published elsewhere in the "open" literature?
3) Are paradigmatic shifts occurring over time?

Individuals interested in this field of investigation are encouraged to correspond with the author. Comments and suggestions will be appreciated.

References

1. Hester Hoffman, "The Graduate Thesis in Library Science," Master's thesis, University of Chicago, 1941, p. 7.

SUMMARY OF CONFERENCE PAPERS

By Gary R. Purcell

The theme of the conference, "Communicating Public Access to Government Information," is addressed clearly in the preface and each of the eight chapters of this book. The variety of topics dealt with enables the reader to consider the theme from several different vantage points. As a result, the issue of public access can be observed as a multifaceted problem, one which should be of major concern to agencies and individuals who produce, disseminate, and service government-produced information. The chapters are oriented toward such issues as: (1) public policy regarding the disclosure and distribution of government information; (2) the appropriate role of librarians and other information professionals in protecting the public's right to information; (3) the knowledge of nonprint formats required for librarians to assist users in gaining access to government information; and (4) the level of competency displayed by documents librarians who provide service to published government information sources. This summary will attempt to show the relationships among the chapters and to suggest their implications for the profession and for library education.

Three of the chapters are written by individuals who represent the federal or provincial government agencies of the U.S. or Canada that produce, disseminate and/or service government information. The first of these authors, Bernadine Hoduski, a member of the Joint Committee on Printing of the U.S. Congress, proposes that librarians play a more active role in influencing government and the private sector to improve the scope and methods of the dissemination of information. Her point is that librarians have great credibility with the decision-makers who determine public information policy because their objectives are not perceived as being self-serving. The library profession is regarded as serving the public interest as a result of its concern with the public's right to continued and increased access to government information. Ms. Hoduski supports her position with examples of the successes librarians have had in influencing information policy in the public and private sectors.

A second government agency official represented by a chapter in this book is Joseph Caponio, Acting Director of the National Technical Information Service (NTIS). He describes current and planned NTIS information services and some of the issues the agency faces at present. His chapter provides a valuable overview of the activities of an agency that plays a central role in the chain of information transfer, especially in scientific and technical fields. During the past few years, NTIS has assumed an increasingly active role in the transfer of scientific and commercial information, including the responsibility for licensing inventions developed through public funding. Some of the agency's newest services have been assumed from those terminated by other agencies (e.g., the Smithsonian Science Information Exchange); others are a result of newly developed service concepts. Dr. Caponio's comments give readers a useful view of an information-dissemination agency that is actively seeking to expand its service responsiblities.

The third representative of a government agency, Brian Land, Director of the Ontario Legislative Library, Research and Information Services, recounts the history of efforts in the Canadian House of Commons to legislate a Freedom of Information Act. This chapter is noteworthy for several reasons, among which are its narrative of efforts in Canada to secure the public's right of access to government information and its valuable comparisons between the major provisions of the proposed act of the House of Commons of Canada and the existing U.S. Freedom of Information Act. Through this comparison, various concepts of "the public's right to know" are identified, resulting in an increased understanding of alternative responses to the freedom of information issue.

Although the content and objectives of each of these chapters are different, at least two common themes can be detected. One is that government in a free society, both for political and commercial reasons, is generally committed to the exchange of information. The second is that government is somewhat ambivalent about how far to go in the implementation of this concept. It appears to be willing to go further in the dissemination of information for commercial purposes than for political purposes, but there are distinct pressures pulling in each direction. The existence of this ambivalence gives added strength to the recommendation by Ms. Hoduski that librarians, who are committed to extending public access to information, work actively to increase the range of government information available to citizens.

Two of the chapters are concerned with types of information resources that are nontraditional and hence have been neglected by most librarians. Each of the authors plays an advocacy role, arguing that librarians should be better informed and more knowledgeable about these information formats. Kathleen M. Heim, from the library school at the University of Illinois, addresses the topic of public access to machine-readable, statistical data files (MRDF). She outlines the problems at the federal level in the United States of identifying the existence of, and obtaining access to, machine-readable statistical data files. She also suggests that librarians can function effectively as brokers of machine-readable information and proposes ways whereby this can be done at different levels. Her chapter delineates an expanded role for librarians in dealing with a format which is still foreign to most of them. The chapter makes a strong case for the position that, with ever-increasing amounts of information produced and disseminated by the government in machine-readable form, it is imperative that librarians become acquainted with this format and utilize it extensively.

The second of these chapters deals with government-produced maps. Charles Seavey, formerly Documents and Map Librarian at the University of New Mexico, gives the reader an overview of the characteristics of maps produced and distributed by government agencies. He points out that a high percentage of all maps produced in the world are issued by government agencies, which in effect makes the acquisition of, and public access to, maps a public documents problem. He also notes that the development and management of map collections are far less well understood by librarians than the development and management of more conventional types of materials. This generally results in less satisfactory service for maps than for other resources. In order to be effective in providing public access to the information found in maps, librarians must seek to increase their understanding of this format.

The two chapters mentioned above deal with formats with which most librarians are not comfortable. Seavey's observation that most librarians are cartographically illiterate could also apply analogously to the level of literacy with respect to machine-readable data files. Because of the importance of these two types of information formats and because ever-increasing amounts of information are being produced and distributed in each of them, it is very important that library educators examine their curricula to determine if librarians are being prepared adequately to provide public access to information appearing in these formats. Further, continuing education programs are called for and should be directed to librarians who are not specialists in the use of either of these formats. Serious deficiencies appear to exist in the profession's overall knowledge of information found in maps and in machine-readable data files, and each of these chapters makes a strong case for addressing them.

Two chapters are reports of research concerned with some aspect of government documents service. John Richardson, Jr., of the library school at UCLA, reports on a study of research activity concerned with government documents in specialization papers, theses, and dissertations prepared in ALA-accredited library schools. The results of this report show which schools have fostered research in government documents and where the subject priorities for this research have been placed. One practical result of this research has been to identify those schools having a strong interest in government publications. Another has been to chart the subject emphasis in government documents research over the past several years.

The second of the two research reports is a study, conducted by Peter Hernon of the library school at Simmons College and Charles McClure of the library school at the University of Oklahoma, of reference service for users of government publications. This report provides some startling information about the limited effectiveness of depository libraries in providing accurate and timely information derived from depository collections. The initial purpose of the depository system was to deliver government information to the citizens of the United States, and thus make the information more readily accessible. If, for one reason or another, the depository system is ineffective in making information accessible, then the goal is subverted. This study indicates that there may be serious limitations to the ability of depository libraries to provide an acceptable level of information service. The implications of these limitations for public access to government information are clear. They apply not only to depository libraries but also to the library education programs responsible for preparing documents librarians. The results of this study should be given careful consideration by all who are engaged in providing public access to government information.

One chapter is an account of the use of government-produced information for the study of public policy issues. This report is concerned with public policy decisions and the government's position with regard to American Indians. Michael Tate, of the Department of History of the University of Nebraska (Omaha), traces the history of public policy toward the Indian population of the Untied States, as reflected in official government publications. He also demonstrates how the contents of publications affect future policy decisions, which themselves result in publications that continue to affect policy decisions, thus creating a cyclical effect. His chapter is also a demonstration of how the official record of the activities and operations of government is used by the research community. Professor Tate's report is that of a researcher who must rely on the accumulated record of official government publications, and thus it shows the acute need of historians for ready access to this type of information.

As noted above, the theme of the conference papers reported in the chapters of this book is "Communicating Public Access to Government Information." The authors' tacit assumption is that public access can be improved in various ways. Improvements can be made through: (1) a more active role by librarians and by government information agencies; (2) improved knowledge and understanding of the types of resources through which information is transmitted; (3) better research about government documents and documents librarianship, and subsequent action based on the research; and (4) improvement in the quality of service provided by service points in the system designed for the distribution of government publications. These several points can be found in each of the chapters, and documents librarians should give careful consideration to the conclusions presented in the papers at this conference.

BIBLIOGRAPHY

Articles

Armstrong, Ann, and Russell, Judith C. "Public Access." *Information World* 1 (October 1979): 1 and 11.

Bergen, Dan. "The Communication System of the Social Sciences." *College and Research Libraries* 28 (July 1967): 239-252.

"Bibliographical Services in the Social Sciences." *Library Quarterly* 20 (April 1950): 79-100.

"Bills Threaten Indian Rights." *Indian Natural Resources* (December 1977): 7.

Brittain, J.M. "Information Services and the Structure of Knowledge in the Social Sciences." *International Social Science Journal* 31 (1979): 712.

———, and Roberts, S.A. "Information Services in the Social Sciences: Development and Rationalization." *International Social Science Journal* 28 (1976): 835.

Chaput, Donald. "Generals, Indian Agents, Politicians: The Doolittle Survey of 1865." *Western Historical Quarterly* 3 (July 1972): 269-282.

Childers, Thomas. "The Test of Reference." *Library Journal* 105 (April 15, 1980): 924-928.

———. "Trends in Public Library I & R Services." *Library Journal* 104 (October 1, 1979): 2035-2039.

Clark, Barton M. "Social Science Data Archives and Libraries: A View to the Future." *Library Trends* 30 (Winter 1982): 505-509.

Dodd, Sue A. "Toward Integration of Catalog Records on Social Science Machine-Readable Data Files into Existing Bibliographic Utilities: A Commentary." *Library Trends* 30 (Winter 1982): 335-361.

Duncan, Joseph W. "Accessing Social Statistics." *Library Trends* 30 (Winter 1982): 363-376.

Earle, Penelope, and Vickery, B.C. "Social Science Literature Use in the UK as Indicated by Citations." *Journal of Documentation* 25 (June 1969): 123-141.

Funke, Karl A. "Educational Assistance and Employment Preference: Who Is An Indian." *American Indian Law Review* 4 (no. 1): 1-45.

Glaspell, Kate Eldridge. "Incidents in the Life of a Pioneer." *North Dakota Historical Quarterly* 8 (1941): 187-188.

Hernon, Peter. "Documents Librarianship in the 1980s: Current Issues and Trends in Research." *Government Publications Review* 9 (1982): 99-120.

Jones, Ray. "The Data Library in the University of Florida Libraries." *Library Trends* 30 (Winter 1982): 395.

Kelsey, Harry. "The Doolittle Report of 1867: Its Preparation and Shortcomings." *Arizona and the West* 17 (Summer 1975): 107-120.

Kickingbird, Kirke. "The American Indian Policy Review Commission: A Prospect for Future Change in Federal Indian Policy." *American Indian Law Review* 3 (1975): 243-253.

Larsgaard, Mary. "Education for Map Librarianship." *Library Trends* 29 (Winter 1981): 499-511.

Lawson, Michael L. "How the Bureau of Indian Affairs Discourages Historical Research." *Indian Historian* 10 (Fall 1977): 25-27.

Line, Maurice B. "Information Requirements in the Social Sciences: Some Preliminary Considerations." *Journal of Librarianship* 1 (January 1969): 1-19.

———. "Information Uses and Needs of Social Scientists: An Overview of INFOSS." *Aslib Proceedings* 23 (September 1971): 412-434.

Meister, Cary W. "The Misleading Nature of Data in the Bureau of the Census Subject Report on 1970 American Indian Population." *Indian Historian* 11 (December 1978): 12-19.

Nebraska Indian Commission Newsletter 6 (September 1981): 5.

Nebraska Indian Territory News 3 (July-August 1978): 1.

Riley, Tom. "A Comparison of Information Laws in the U.S. and Canada." *Journal of Media Law and Practice* 2 (September 1981): 192.

Ristow, Walter W. "The Emergence of Maps in Libraries." *Special Libraries* 58 (July-August 1967): 400-419.

Robbin, Alice. "The Pre-Acquisition Process: A Strategy for Locating and Acquiring Machine-Readable Data." *Drexel Library Quarterly* 13 (January 1977): 21-42.

———. "Strategies for Improving Utilization of Computerized Statistical Data by the Social Scientific Community." *Social Science Information Studies* 1 (1981): 89-109.

Rowe, Judith S. "Expanding Social Science Reference Service to Meet the Needs of Patrons More Adequately." *Library Trends* 30 (Winter 1982): 327-334.

Seavey, Charles A. "Collection Development for Government Map Collections." *Government Publications Review* 8A (1981): 17-29.

Smalley, Topsy N. "Political Science: The Discipline, the Literature, and the Library." *Libri* 30 (1980): 33-52.

Simmons, James L. "One Little, Two Little, Three Little Indians: Counting American Indians in Urban Society." *Human Organization* 36 (Spring 1977): 76-79.

Stefon, Frederick J. "Significance of the Meriam Report of 1928." *Indian Historian* 7 (Summer 1975):2-7.

Tate, Michael L. "Red Power: Government Publications and the Rising Indian Activism of the 1970s." *Government Publications Review* 8 (1981): 499-518.

Books

American Library Association. *Anglo-American Cataloging Rules.* 2nd ed. Chicago: ALA, 1978.

American Psychological Association. *Reports of the American Psychological Association's Project on Scientific Information Exchange in Psychology.* Washington, D.C.: APA, 1965.

Association of Canadian Map Libraries. *Proceedings.* 1967.

Barsh, Russell Lawrence and Henderson, James Youngblood. *The Road: Indian Tribes and Political Liberty.* Berkeley: University of California Press, 1980.

Boruch, Robert F.; Cordray, David S.; and Wortman, Paul M. *Reanalyzing Program Evaluations: Policies and Practices for Secondary Analysis of Social and Educational Programs.* San Francisco: Jossey-Bass, 1981.

Brittain, J.M. *Information and Its Users.* Claverton Down, Bath: Bath University Press.

Burnette, Robert and Koster, John. *The Road to Wounded Knee.* New York: Bantam Books, 1974.

Crecine, John P. *Research in Public Policy Analysis and Management: Basic Theory, Methods, and Perspectives.* Greenwich, CT: JAI Press, 1981.

Crowley, Terence, and Childers, Thomas. *Information Service in Public Libraries: Two Studies.* Metuchen, N.J.: Scarecrow, 1971.

Durant, Will, and Durant, Ariel. *The Story of Civilization, Part VII: The Age of Reason Begins.* New York: Simon and Schuster, 1961.

Foskett, D. J. *Classification and Indexing in the Social Sciences.* London: Butterworths, 1974.

Freides, Thelma. *Literature and Bibliography of the Social Sciences.* Los Angeles: Melville Publishing, 1973.

Hernon, Peter, and Purcell, Gary R. *Developing Collections of U.S. Government Publications.* Greenwich, CT: JAI Press, forthcoming.

Hoselitz, Bert F. *A Reader's Guide to the Social Sciences.* New York: The Free Press, 1970.

Investigation into Information Requirements of the Social Sciences. Research Report No. 1. Vol. 1. Text by Maurice B. Line. Bath, England: Bath University of Technology, University Library, May 1971.

Johansen, Bruce, and Maetas, Robert. *Wasi' chu: The Continuing Indian Wars.* New York: Monthly Review Press, 1979.

Kruzas, Anthony T. *Encyclopedia of Information Systems and Services.* Detroit: Gale, 1980.

144   Bibliography

Madge, John. *The Tools of Social Sciences*. London: Longmans, Green, 1953.
McCamus, John D. *Freedom of Information: Canadian Perspectives*. Toronto: Butterworths, 1981.
McClure, Charles R., and Hernon, Peter. *Improving the Quality of Reference Service for Government Publications*. Chicago: ALA, forthcoming.
McLuhan, Marshall. *Understanding Media*. New York: McGraw-Hill, 1964.
Otis, D.S. *The Dawes Severalty Act and the Allotment of Indian Lands*. Edited by Francis Paul Prucha. Norman: University of Oklahoma Press, 1973.
Parman, Donald L. *The Navajos and the New Deal*. New Haven: Yale University Press, 1976.
The Problem of Indian Administration. Baltimore: Johns Hopkins Press, 1928.
Ristow, Walter W. *The Emergence of Maps in Libraries*. Hamden, Conn.: Linnet Books, 1980.
Taylor, Graham D. *The New Deal and American Indian Tribalism: The Administration of the Indian Reorganization Act, 1934-1945*. Lincoln: University of Nebraska Press, 1980.
Thrower, Norman J.W. *Maps and Man*. Englewood Cliffs, N.J.: Prentice-Hall, 1972.
University of Northern Iowa. *Map Collection Manual*. 1979.
Wasserman, Paul. *Statistics Sources*. 7th ed. Detroit: Gale, 1982.
Webb, Eugene et al. *Unobtrusive Measures*. Chicago: Rand McNally, 1966.
Weber, George H., and McCall, George J. *Social Scientists as Advocates: Views from the Applied Disciplines*. Beverly Hills, CA: Sage, 1978.
White, Carl M. et al. *Sources of Information in the Social Sciences: A Guide to the Literature*. 2nd ed. Chicago: ALA, 1973.

Dissertations and Theses

Heim, Kathleen M. "Social Science Data Archives: A User Study." Ph.D. dissertation, University of Wisconsin-Madison, 1980.
Hoffman, Hester, "The Graduate Thesis in Library Science." Master's thesis, University of Chicago. 1941.
Jirjees, Jassim Muhammad. "The Accuracy of Selected Northeastern College Library Reference/Information Telephone Services in Responding to Factual Inquiries." Ph.D. dissertation, Rutgers University, 1981.
Myers, Marcia Jean. "The Effectiveness of Telephone Reference/Information Services in Academic Libraries in the Southeast." Ph.D. dissertation, Florida State University, 1979.
Vondran, Jr., Raymond F. "The Effect of Method of Research on the Information Seeking Behavior of Academic Historians." Ph.D. dissertation, University of Wisconsin-Madison, 1976.
White, Howard D. "Social Science Data Sets: A Study for Librarians." Ph.D. dissertation, University of California, Berkeley, 1974.

Government Publications

Canada

Cabinet. *Directive Number 45: Notices of Motion for the Production of Papers*. Ottawa, 1973.

Department of the Secretary of State. *Legislation on Public Access to Government Documents.* Ottawa: Supply and Services Canada, 1977.

Laws, Statutes, etc. *Canadian Human Rights Act.* Ottawa, 1977.

————. Bills of the House of Commons. *Bill C-15, An Act to Extend the Present Laws of Canada That Provide Access to Information under the Control of the Government of Canada and to Amend the Canada Evidence Act, the Federal Court Act and the Statutory Instruments Act.* The Hon. Walter Baker. 1st reading, 24 October 1979.

————.————. *Bill C-43, An Act To Enact the Access to Information Act and the Privacy Act, to Amend the Federal Court Act and the Canadian Evidence Act, and to Amend Certain Other Acts in Consequence Thereof.* The Hon. Francis Fox. 1st reading, 17 July 1980.

————.————. *Bill C-225, An Act Respecting the Right of the Public to Information Concerning the Public Business.* Gerald W. Baldwin. 1st reading, 15 October 1974.

Parliament. House of Commons. *Journals.* 30th Parliament. 1st reading, 12 February 1976.

————.————. Standing Committee on Justice and Legal Affairs. *Minutes of Proceedings and Evidence.* 32nd Parliament. 1st session, no. 37, 2 June 1981. Ottawa, 1981; *Proceedings,* no. 46, 26 June 1981; no. 47, 30 June 1981; no. 38, 4 June 1981; no. 39, 9 June 1981; no. 21, 24 March 1981; no. 40, 11 June 1981; no. 54, 19 November 1981; and no. 42, 17 June 1981.

————.————. Standing Joint Committee on Regulations and Other Statutory Instruments. *Fifth Report Journals.* 30th Parliament. 3rd session, 28 June 1978.

Task Force on Government Information. *To Know and Be Known: Report.* Vols. 1 and 2. Ottawa: Queen's Printer, 1969.

Organisation for Economic Cooperation and Development

The Utilisation of the Social Sciences in Policy Making in the United States. Paris: OECD, 1980.

United States

Annual Report of the Board of Indian Commissioners to the Secretary of Interior for the Fiscal Year Ended June 30, 1926. Washington: GPO, 1926.

Bureau of the Census. *Census of Population 1970. Subject Reports, Final Report PC (2)-1F. American Indians.* Washington: GPO, 1973.

Congress. Senate. *Conditions of the Indian Tribes. Report of the Joint Special Committee Appointed under Joint Resolution of March 3, 1865. Senate Report 156.* 39th Cong., 2nd sess., 1867.

————.————. *Freedom of Information Reform Act. S. 1730.* 97th Cong., 1st sess., 1981.

————.————. *Hearings on S.J. Res. 133 before the Subcommittee on Indian Affairs of the Senate Committee on Interior and Insular Affairs.* 93rd Cong., 1st sess., 1973.

———. ——— *Review of Conditions of the Indians in the United States. Hearings before the Committee on Indian Affairs. S. Res. 78 and 308.* 71st Cong., 2nd sess., 1930.

———. ———. *Survey of Conditions among the Indians of the United States, Supplementary Report. Report No. 310, Pt. 2,* 78th Cong., 2nd sess., 1944.

———. ———. *Survey of Conditions of the Indians in the United States. Hearings before the Committee on Indian Affairs.* 70th-78th Congresses, 1928-1943 (41 parts).

Cutter, Charles Ammi. "Rules for a Dictionary Catalog." In U.S. Bureau of Education, *Special Report on Public Libraries, Part II.* 4th ed. 1904.

Department of Commerce. National Technical Information Service and Office of Federal Statistical Policy and Standards. *Directory of Federal Statistical Data Files.* Springfield, Virginia: NTIS, PB 81-133175.

———. Office of Federal Statistical Policy and Standards. *A Framework for Planning U.S. Federal Statistics for the 1980s.* Washington, D.C.: GPO, 1978.

"Federal Statistical Data File Catalogs and Directories." *Statistical Reporter.* March 1981, pp. 341-344.

Ferguson, Jack. *Specialized Social Science Information Services in the United States.* Clearinghouse for Federal Scientific and Technical Information, PB 167 841.

"Freedom of Information Act," 5 *United States Code* 552 (1966).

The Indian Problem. Resolution of the Committee of One Hundred Appointed by the Secretary of the Interior and a Review of the Indian Problem, January 7, 1924. Washington, D.C.: GPO. 1924.

Lanagona, Stephen A. "A Statistical Profile of the Indian: The Lack of Numbers." In *Toward Economic Development for Native American Communities.* Washington, D.C.: GPO, 1969.

Library of Congress. *Subject Headings.* 1st ed. Washington, D.C.: The Library, 1909-1914.

National Center for Education Statistics. *Education Statistics: Colleges and Universities, 1979-1980.* Washington, D.C.: GPO. 1981.

National Research Council. Committee on Information in the Behavioral Sciences. *Communication System and Resources in the Behavioral Sciences.* Washington, D.C.: National Science Academy, 1967.

National Research Council. Study Project on Social Research and Development. *The Federal Investment in Knowledge of Social Problems* (n.d.)

———. ———. *The Funding of Social Knowledge Production and Application* (n.d.)

———. ———. *Studies in the Management of Social R & D* (n.d.).

———. ———. *Knowledge and Policy* (n.d.).

———. ———. *The Uses of Basic Research* (n.d.).

Public Law 93-580. "Joint Resolution to Provide for the Establishment of the American Indian Policy Review Commission, January 2, 1975." *Statutes at Large.* 93rd Cong., 2nd sess.

"Selected Data Access Publications," *Statistical Reporter.* March 1981, pp. 341-344.

Sprehe, J. Timothy. "A Federal Policy for Improving Data Access and User Services." *Statistical Reporter.* March 1981, pp. 323-341.

Triplett, Myra L. "The Role of Interagency Committees in Statistical Policy Coordination," *Statistical Reporter.* October 1980, p.1.

Tyler, S. Lyman. "A History of Indian Policy." Department of the Interior. Bureau of Indian Affairs. Washington, D.C.: 1973.

Worldwide Directory of National Earth Science Agencies and Related International Organizations. U.S. Geological Survey Circular 834. Reston, VA: The Survey, 1981.

Newsletters and Newspapers

Globe and Mail (Toronto), 11 December 1981; 3 February 1982; and 12 February 1982.

IASIST Newsletter.

Wassaja, January-February 1975, p. 19; June 1975, p. 2; September 1976, p. 2; and November-December 1976, p. 2.

Personal Correspondence

Letter from Michael L. Lawson (Rights Protection Branch of the Aberdeen Area Office of the BIA, Aberdeen, South Dakota), September 28, 1981.

Unpublished Papers

Bisco, Ralph L. "Draft (Second Version) of a Proposal for Support of CSSDA for Five Years Beginning July 1968." Mimeographed. 20 November 1967.

Cherns, Jack. "Government Publishing—An Overview." Paper given to International Federation of Library Associations and Institutions. 44th Cong. Paper No. 16/Op/1E, 1978.

NASA Report, 1981?, held by Charles A. Seavey.

Radlinski, William A. "Federal Mapping and Charting in the United States." Paper presented at the 9th International Conference on Cartography, 26 July 1978, at the University of Maryland, College Park.

Seavey, Charles A. "Developing the Academic Map Collection." Paper presented at the ACRL National Conference, Minneapolis, Minnesota, October 1981.

Miscellaneous

Canadian Library Association. *Brief. App. "JLA-10."*

Conversation with Gary North, Chief of Information and Data Services, U.S. Geological Survey, 26 March 1982.

Information from Dwight Canfield, Director, U.S. Geological Survey Distribution Center, Denver, Colorado, 11 February 1982.

CONTRIBUTORS

Peter Hernon, who received his Ph.D. degree from Indiana University in 1978, teaches at the Graduate School of Library and Information Science, Simmons College, Boston. His primary concerns are in the areas of government publications, reference methods and services, and the literature of the social sciences. He is the author of numerous books and articles in the documents field. Examples of his works include: *Use of Government Publications by Social Scientists* (Norwood, N.J.: Ablex Publishing Corp., 1979), *Microforms and Government Information* (Westport, CT: Microform Review, 1981), and *Developing Collections of U.S. Government Publications* (Greenwich, CT: JAI Press, forthcoming).

Joseph F. Caponio is Acting Director of the National Technical Information Service (NTIS). Prior to assuming that position, he was the Deputy Director.

Before joining NTIS, Dr. Caponio was Acting Director of the Environmental Data and Information Service of the National Oceanographic and Atmospheric Administration. Prior to that he was with the National Agricultural Library.

Dr. Caponio, a biochemist, is a member of the American Chemical Society, the American Society for Information Science, and is a Fellow of the American Association for the Advancement of Science.

Kathleen M. Heim, who received her Ph.D. degree from the University of Wisconsin in 1980, is Associate Professor, Graduate School of Library and Information Science, University of Illinois, Urbana. She teaches two courses relating to government publications and is editor of *RQ*. Her most recent publication is in the Winter 1982 issue of *Library Trends*, which is devoted to data libraries and the social sciences.

Bernadine E. Abbott Hoduski is Professional Staff Member for Library and Distribution Services, the Joint Committee on Printing, U.S. Congress. She also teaches a course on government information at the library school, Catholic University. Prior to assuming her position with the Joint Committee on Printing, she was Head Librarian, U.S. Environmental Protection Agency, Kansas City, Missouri. She received her M.A. in librarianship in 1965 from the University of Denver (Colorado).

Ms. Hoduski, who is active in various professional associations, was one of the founders of the Government Documents Round Table (GODORT) of the American Library Association. She was awarded the James Bennett Childs Award for "distinguished contributions to documents librarianship." She has served on the editorial board of *Government Publications Review* since the journal's inception, and has written a number of articles and papers in the documents field. Ms. Hoduski was elected Secretary for the International Federation of Library Associations and Institutions, Official Publications Committee, in 1981. On behalf of IFLA, she has organized an international meeting of government publishers, librarians, and users in Saratoga Springs, New York, from August 29 to September 1, 1982.

R. Brian Land has been the Director of the Ontario Legislative Library, Research and Information Services, in Toronto since September 1978. He also holds the rank of Professor of Library Science, University of Toronto, where he teaches courses in government publications and in business information sources.

Land has served as Dean of Library Science, University of Toronto (1964-72), as Executive Assistant to the Minister of Finance, Ottawa (1963-64), as Assistant and Associate Chief Librarian, University of Toronto (1959-63), and as Assistant and Associate Editor of *Canadian Business* magazine (1957-59).

A native of Niagara Falls, Ontario, Professor Land holds graduate degrees in political science and library science from the University of Toronto. He is the author of numerous articles and of *Sources of Information for Canadian Business* (3rd ed., 1978) and is the editor of the *Directory of Associations in Canada* (4th ed., 1982). He is also the Canadian Correspondent for the *ALA Yearbook*.

Professor Land has been active in the work of professional associations and has served as President of the Canadian Library Association, the Canadian Association of Library Schools, the Association of American Library Schools and the Institute of Professional Librarians of Ontario. He has also served as Chairman of the ALA Committee on Accreditation and as a Commissioner of the Canadian Radio-television and Telecommunications Commission.

Charles R. McClure is Associate Professor at the School of Library Science, University of Oklahoma. He received his Ph.D. in Library and Information Services from Rutgers University. He has published a number of articles related to government publications and recently was issue editor and contributor to a theme issue, "Technology Applications for Government Documents Collections," appearing in *Government Publications Review*. He is co-authoring a monograph, *Improving the Quality of Reference Service for Government Publications*, with Peter Hernon, which will be published by the American Library Association in early 1983.

Gary R. Purcell is Professor, Graduate School of Library and Information Science, University of Tennessee, Knoxville. He received his MLS from the University of Washington and the Ph.D. in Library and Information Science from Case Western Reserve University. In addition, he holds an M.A. in Political Science from Case Western Reserve. Dr. Purcell has taught courses in public documents at Western Michigan University and Case Western Reserve University, as well as the University of Tennessee. He has been the President of the Association of American Library Schools and the Tennessee Library Association. He has written or co-written several articles concerned with government publications. He co-authored (with Peter Hernon) *Developing Collections of U.S. Government Publications*. He also co-edited the special issue of *Government Publications Review* devoted to collection development for government publications (8A, Numbers 1 and 2, 1981).

John V. Richardson, Jr. is currently Assistant Professor in the Graduate School of Library and Information Science, University of California, Los Angeles.

He holds a B.A. in Sociology from Ohio State University (1971), an M.L.S. from Vanderbilt University, Peabody College (1972), and a Ph.D. degree from Indiana University (1978). His doctoral dissertation has been published as *The Spirit of Inquiry in Library Science*, ACRL Publications in Librarianship, No. 42 (Chicago: American Library Association, 1982). He has taught at Indiana University and the University of Kentucky.

As a documents librarian at the University of Kentucky, he initiated and developed a monthly checklist of state publications and wrote about state government publications.

At Indiana University, he became involved with *Government Publications Review*, first as a book reviewer and then as column editor of "Theses in Documents." He presently serves on the editorial board. Along with Peter Hernon and others, he co-authored *Municipal Government Reference Sources* (New York: Bowker, 1978).

His numerous awards and honors include several Faculty Research Grants from UCLA's Academic Senate, a Newberry Summer Fellowship (1982), an entry in *Who's Who in Library and Information Services* (1982), U.S. Jaycees Outstanding Young Man (1979), and Beta Phi Mu (1973).

At UCLA, he continues to write, teach, and supervise research in the area of government publications. Among his recent articles are "The United States Government as Publisher Since the Roosevelt Administration" (1982), "The Bibliographic Organization of Federal Depository Collections" (1980), and "The Federal Depository Library System" (1978). He is currently working on a book based on the paper published herein and is collecting material for an article with Gail Nelson on the development of the Superintendent of Documents Classification scheme.

Beginning with the fall 1982 semester, **Charles A. Seavey** will be a doctoral student at the Library School, University of Wisconsin, Madison. Previously, he was head of the Government Publications and Maps Department, University of New Mexico, Albuquerque. Mr. Seavey, who has been active in both the documents and maps fields, has written an article on collection development for government map collections (*Government Publications Review*, 8A, 1981, 17-29) and is currently editing a special issue of *Government Publications Review* devoted to government map collections. He has also delivered a paper on "Developing the Academic Map Collection" at the ACRL National Conference, Minneapolis, Minnesota, 1981.

Michael L. Tate, Associate Professor of History at the University of Nebraska at Omaha, received his Ph.D. in American Frontier and American Indian history from the University of Toledo in 1974. He has published numerous articles on these subjects in sources such as *Journal of the West, Great Plains Journal, American Indian Quarterly, The Americas: A Quarterly Review of Inter-American Cultural History, Chronicles of Oklahoma, Arizona and the West, Red River Valley Historical Review, Teaching History,* and *Government Publications Review*. He has also published chapters in several books and articles in several encyclopedias.

In his work with the American Indian Center of Omaha, Dr. Tate has taped over sixty hours of oral history interviews with Native Americans, as well as over one hundred hours of interviews on Great Plains experiences from 1900-1940. He has simultaneously served as a Contributing Editor to *American Indian Quarterly* and an Executive Editor of *Government Publications Review*.

Dr. Tate is currently working on a book length treatment of the Comanche and Kiowa tribes, and a second manuscript dramatizing the history of American Indians in the United States Army. He has also contracted with Scarecrow Press for a 350-page annotated bibliography on the Indians of Texas for the "Native American Bibliography Series.